DATE DUE

S

DEC 1 2 2001			
GAYLORD			PRINTED IN U.S.A.

The Netherlands

The Netherlands

BY MARTIN HINTZ

4/01 J 914.92

Enchantment of the World
Second Series

Children's Press®

A Division of Grolier Publishing

NEW YORK   LONDON   HONG KONG   SYDNEY
DANBURY, CONNECTICUT

Frontispiece: Windmills in a pasture at Leidschendam

Consultant: Ruth Mitchell-Pitts, Ph.D., Administrative Director,
Center for European Studies, University of North Carolina at Chapel Hill

Please note: All statistics are as up-to-date as possible at the time of publication.

Visit Children's Press on the Internet: http://publishing.grolier.com

Book Production by Herman Adler Design Group

Library of Congress Cataloging-in-Publication Data

Hintz, Martin
    The Netherlands / by Martin Hintz.
       p. cm. — (Enchantment of the world. Second series)
    Includes bibliographical references and index.
    Summary: Describes the geography, plants and animals, history,
economy, language, religions, culture, and people of The Netherlands.
    ISBN 0-516-20962-0
    1. Netherlands—Juvenile literature. [1. Netherlands.] I. Title.
II. Series.
DJ18.H56 1999
949.2—dc21   98-41700
                                           CIP
                                           AC

GROLIER
PUBLISHING
    2 3 4 5 6 7 8 9 10 R 08 07 06 05 04 03 02 01 00

Acknowledgments

The author would like to thank the many Dutch educators, artists, political leaders, business representatives, and others who provided support in researching *Enchantment of the World: The Netherlands*. Hintz wants to especially express his appreciation to Bram Groeneveld for his assistance, encouragement, and keen observations. This book is for the children of World War II.

Cover photo:
Amsterdam

Contents

Tulip fields in Lisse

Traditional Dutch
clothes

What's in a Name?

8

HOLLAND. THE NETHERLANDS. LOW COUNTRIES. DUTCH. What's with all these names? Do they all mean the same thing? This compact country tucked along Europe's North Sea coast is often called *Holland* by English-speaking people. The Dutch prefer to call their country by its proper name— *Koninkrijk der Nederlanden* (Kingdom of the Netherlands). The short version is *Nederland* (the Netherlands), which means "low land."

Opposite: **A dike built around a Friesland community**

A Dutch girl dressed in traditional clothing

Romans Conquer the Land

The Romans conquered this low, flat land between France and Germany more than 2,000 years ago. They called it *Terra inferior* in Latin, a name that became the "Low Countries" in English. Historically, this territory included Belgium, Luxembourg, and the Netherlands. Every generation or so, wars erupted in the region and borders changed regularly.

In the early 1600s, the northern section of the Low Countries became known as *the Netherlands.* After the Treaty of Utrecht in 1713, the southern Low Countries was called *Belgium. Luxembourg,* which means "little castle," was then a Belgian province.

Geopolitical map of the Netherlands

NETHERLANDS

- ● Cities of over 100,000 people
- ○ Smaller cities and towns
- ◉○ Divisional capitals
- — Canals

0 _____ 40 miles

0 _____ 60 kilometers

NORTH SEA

West Frisian Islands

Waddenzee

Groningen

GRONINGEN

Leeuwarden

FRIESLAND

Assen

DRENTHE

IJsselmeer

NOORD-HOLLAND (Zuider Zee)

FLEVOLAND

Alkmaar

Lelystad

Zwolle

Vechte

Ems

Haarlem

Amsterdam

IJssel

OVERIJSSEL

Deventer

Enschede

ZUID-HOLLAND

Old Rhine

Apeldoorn

GELDERLAND

Leiden

Utrecht

UTRECHT

Lower Rhine

Arnhem

The Hague

Delft

Lek

Nijmegen

Rotterdam

Maas

ZEELAND

Dordrecht

NOORD-BRABANT

's Hertogenbosh

Middelburg

Breda

Tilburg

Eindhoven

Terneuzen

LIMBURG

Rhine

Lys

Brussels

Maastricht

BELGIUM

Meuse

GERMANY

NETHERLANDS

LUXEMBOURG

For a time, Belgium remained separate from the Netherlands. The two were reunited under Netherlands' rule when the French empire of Napoleon Bonaparte was divided in 1815. The Belgians revolted in 1830, splitting away from what they called the *Nederland*. Tiny Luxembourg became a semi-independent grand duchy at the mercy of outside political forces through World War II (1939–1945).

After the revolt, the name the *Netherlands* came into common usage. It indicates a country separate from Belgium and Luxembourg. So now that we've cleared up the origin of the Netherlands, where is Holland?

North and South Provinces

The name *Holland* refers to the country's two western provinces—North Holland and South Holland—though the term is often, and incorrectly, interchanged with the Netherlands. Holland includes the major cities of Amsterdam, Rotterdam, The Hague, Delft, Leiden, and Haarlem, but ten other provinces are also part of the Netherlands.

Now let's move on to *Dutch*. This name refers to the Netherlanders—the people of the Netherlands. *Dutch* is

Dam Square in Amsterdam

Shell Oil World Headquarters in Hofplein plaza, Rotterdam

linguistically related to *deutsch*, the contemporary German word for the German language. In ancient times—in the Germanic origin of today's Dutch, English, and German languages—*deutsch* meant "the people" or "the nation."

All these names don't need to be confusing. The modern, bustling country presents far more than a traditional picture postcard of windmills, cheese, wooden shoes, and tulips. Today's Netherlands is an international crossroads, with several of the world's largest harbors. Its people are resourceful. The small land mass of the Netherlands was limited by the physical barrier of the North Sea. So the Dutch needed to look outside their own land for economic growth. They were eager colonizers, establishing outposts around the world from New York to Indonesia.

Open to Ideas

The Netherlands has always been open to new ideas. Over the centuries, the country has opened its doors and heart to those in need. The Netherlands had a long history as a political misfit. It was a country born in rebellion, standing alone in a Europe of kings and emperors, while its leadership came from the people. This meant that political and cultural freethinkers were usually welcome in the Netherlands and their energy and talent helped the nation grow. Portuguese Jews, Scottish religious dissenters, displaced Ugandans, and Indonesian refugees have all found refuge here. Each contributed to the nation's robust cultural stew.

This openness also made the Netherlands a cultural leader. Its artists and writers have always been allowed to be creative. As a result, this small country has earned regard far beyond its small size. Look at the great works of Rembrandt and Van Gogh. Something in the Dutch soul seems to lend itself to portraying beauty in amazing ways.

Yet what about those traditional postcard images? Okay, the Dutch do make good cheese. The summertime whir of windmill arms is high drama, especially on a cloudless summer afternoon. The tap-tap of the woodcarver's tools is a symphony in the creation of a wooden shoe. The scent of tulips fills the air.

In the Netherlands, so much is packed into such a small, neat package. "Well," the Dutch respond, "that's just the way we are, and we like it."

A traditional clog maker in Amsterdam

The Dutch Created Holland

Landscape of a farm in Graft with sheep grazing in the pasture

"GOD CREATED THE WORLD, BUT THE DUTCH CREATED Holland" is a famous phrase used in the Netherlands. More than two-fifths of the country's land once lay under the ocean or in swamps. To get dry land, the industrious Dutch drained these areas by pumping out the water from behind huge dikes they had built. The drained areas are called *polders*. Today, more than 60 percent of the Dutch people live in these regions.

The lowest part of the country is the Prins Alexander Polder in the west, at 22 feet (6.7 m) below what is called the Normal Amsterdam Level (NAP). The highest point is 1,053 feet (321 m) above the NAP in the south at Vaalser Berg. The borders of the Netherlands, Belgium, and Germany join here.

Opposite: **Oude Harbor**

The Dutch Created Holland **15**

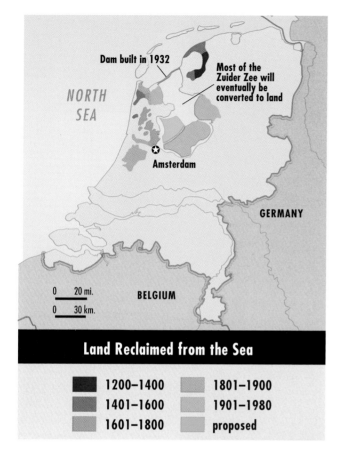

Dam built in 1932

Most of the Zuider Zee will eventually be converted to land

NORTH SEA

Amsterdam

GERMANY

0 20 mi.
0 30 km.

BELGIUM

Land Reclaimed from the Sea

1200–1400	1801–1900
1401–1600	1901–1980
1601–1800	proposed

Water Creates Landscape

In prehistoric times, glaciers and water erosion created the Netherlands' landscape. Tens of thousands of years ago, when the towering sheets of ice began their retreat, they left a wide, boggy bowl-shaped space behind them. At the time, the continent of Europe was still linked to what is now the island of Great Britain. Between 5500 and 3000 B.C., the sea rose and covered the land bridge between the two. For generations, ocean currents then built up sand dunes along the European coast.

For a time, the sand dunes protected the inland ground. But over the

The IJsselmeer

During World War II, many buildings and other structures in the Netherlands were severely damaged. When the conflict ended in 1945, bridges had to be rebuilt, roads and dikes repaired, and polders drained. War equipment, much of it used in the D day invasion of Europe, was put to good use. Wreckage was pushed into place in some dikes to help fill breaches in the system. Once the dikes were back in shape, the seawater was pumped out. Within months, much of the flooded landscape was used for farming again.

centuries, the sea broke through and flooded most of what is now the Netherlands. It was not until the thirteenth century, when powerful windmills were developed for pumping, that it became possible to drain and reclaim this land. Constant vigilance is needed to keep the country dry because the sea is rising about 6 inches (15 cm) a century, due to the melting ice in the earth's polar regions.

A Compact Country

The Netherlands is a compact country with a land area of 16,033 square miles (41,522 sq km), which makes it about twice the size of New Jersey. The country's coastline ranges for 280 miles (451 km). The Netherlands' offshore territorial claims extend 12 nautical miles from the coast, with an exclusive fishing zone of 200 nautical miles.

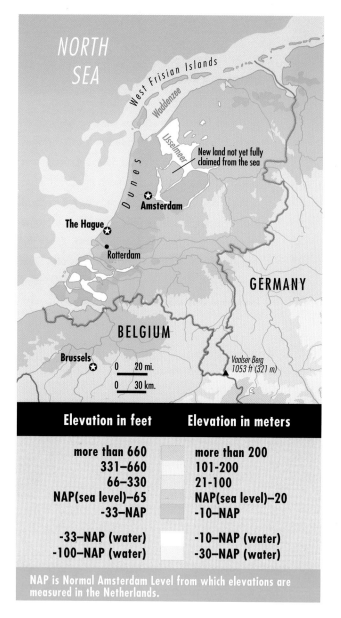

NORTH SEA

West Frisian Islands

Waddenzee

IJsselmeer

New land not yet fully claimed from the sea

Dunes

Amsterdam

The Hague

Rotterdam

GERMANY

BELGIUM

Brussels

0 20 mi.

0 30 km.

Vaalser Berg
1053 ft (321 m)

Elevation in feet		Elevation in meters
more than 660		more than 200
331–660		101-200
66–330		21-100
NAP(sea level)–65		NAP(sea level)–20
-33–NAP		-10–NAP
-33–NAP (water)		-10–NAP (water)
-100–NAP (water)		-30–NAP (water)

NAP is Normal Amsterdam Level from which elevations are measured in the Netherlands.

Topographical map of the Netherlands

The Netherlands' neighbor to the south is Belgium, with a 280-mile (450-km) border. On the east is Germany, with a 359-mile (578-km) border. The Zuider Zee, once a large inlet on the North Sea, was separated from the sea in 1932 by a 19-mile (30-km)-long dike, topped with a freeway that connected the provinces of North Holland and Friesland. The project created a vast inland lake called the IJsselmeer and added 549 square miles (1,422 sq km) of land— enough space for a new province called Flevoland.

Four Major Land Areas

The dunes, the polders, the sand plains, and the southern uplands comprise the Netherlands' four major land areas. The dunes consist of grass-covered sandy ridges along the North Sea coast and make up the West Frisian Islands. Rivers pour into the sea in the south, breaking up the coastal dunes. The polders are wide fertile areas as flat as the proverbial pancake. They lie below sea level, protected by the dikes. Marshy islands and deltas formed by the Maas and Schelde Rivers make up polders in the south where high dams

A polder in winter

prevent flooding. During good weather, massive floodgates are opened to allow saltwater and tides to enter a natural preserve that protects the rare ecology of the region. In storms, the floodgates are shut.

The rolling sand plains are no more than 100 feet (30 m) above sea level. Fruit is grown in the eastern plains, with forests spreading their thick, leafy arms over much of the landscape. Canals connect the rivers here to create an extensive transport web. The highest site in the Netherlands is at Vaalser Berg in the Southern Uplands near the industrial city of Maastricht. The Uplands' sandy soil needs fertilizer to grow crops, but it has luscious grass for grazing cattle.

Geographical Features

Area: 16,033 square miles (41,522 sq km)

Largest City: Amsterdam

Highest Elevation: Vaalser Berg, 1,053 feet (321 m) above sea level

Lowest Elevation: Prins Alexander Polder, 22 feet (6.7 m) below sea level

Longest River: Rhine (part): 820 miles (1,320 kilometers)

Lowest Average Temperature: 37°F (3°C) in January

Highest Average Temperature: 62°F (17°C) in July

Average Annual Rainfall: 29 inches (74 cm)

The sea makes the Netherlands' weather damp but mild, like much of Western Europe. Winters are generally moderate without much snow or frost but heavy fog and dark, overcast skies are common. Summers, on the other hand, are pleasant and comfortable, with sunny skies and gentle breezes. However, sudden showers can fall, so wise Dutch walkers always carry umbrellas. Temperatures range from 60°F to 65°F (16°C to 18°C) in the summer and around 30°F to 35°F (-1°C to 1.7°C) in the winter. Since this small nation has no

The Dutch keep their umbrellas handy because sudden showers are frequent.

geographical barriers except the sea, the climate varies little from one area to another. The Netherlands gets 25 to 30 inches (63 to 76 cm) of rain and snow each year.

Dealing with floodwater is a constant challenge in the Netherlands. Raging North Sea storms can damage the extensive system of dikes and the environmentally fragile dunes that protect the coast. It is difficult to find a safe, high-and-dry place quickly if a dike breaks. Most of the country's larger natural lakes have been pumped dry, but the delta redevelopment program and the reclamation of the Zuider Zee have created numerous new freshwater lakes.

The Best Help

The early Dutch were wise businesspeople. They sought out the best navigators and ship captains to help them open new markets. English explorer Henry Hudson was hired by the Dutch East India Company to search for a passage to the Far East in 1609. He left Amsterdam in April of that year on his ship, the *Half Moon*, with a crew of Dutch and English sailors. Due to storms and a mutiny, Hudson changed direction and sailed directly west. He found the coast of North America and anchored in the lower bay of New York.

Using small boats to sail up a wide, clear river, Hudson and his men got as far as what is now Troy, New York. A crew member named Robert Juet wrote a detailed description of this adventure along the river that would eventually bear his captain's name.

The *Half Moon* sailed for England in October, planning to continue on to the Netherlands. Once at Dartmouth, however, Hudson was warned not to work for the Dutch any more, so he left the ship. But his reports and charts helped the Dutch East India Company establish settlements in Albany and New Amsterdam (New York).

Rivers are important to the Netherlands, keeping saltwater at bay and ensuring a steady flow of freshwater. The Rhine River, which flows from Germany near the city of Nijmegen in the Netherlands, eventually splits in half. A main channel called the Waal continues on to the southwestern part of the Netherlands in the Delta region of islands and inlets. A southern channel called the Lower Rhine flows westward, its name changing to the Lek and then to the Nieuwe Maas. This river

The Nieuwe Maas River is busy with industrial activity.

Windmill Sails Go 'Round and 'Round

Windmills of all sizes and shape are everywhere in the Netherlands. In Kinderdijk, near Dordrecht, the long, flapping arms of 19 windmills still spin. A century ago, 10,000 windmills pumped water from behind the country's dikes. The advent of steam and electrical power put most of the older windmills out of work. Today, there are only about 1,000 active windmills, but many others have been made into houses or museums.

One such museum is the Molen De Valk in Leiden, a seven-story windmill constructed in 1743. It has a miller's house on the ground floor with side buildings housing tools and machinery. An exhibit shows windmill pieces. The wind pump is on the fourth floor.

eventually reaches the ocean along a waterway dug in 1872 from Rotterdam to the sea. Two other major rivers in the Netherlands are the Maas and the Schelde.

This combination of ocean and inland water systems can be dangerous. Great floods were recorded in 1287, 1404, 1421, 1570, and 1916. In 1953, a combination of broken dikes, floods, and storms caused more than 1,800 deaths in the Netherlands. The famous folktale of a little Dutch boy who stuck his finger in a hole in a dike, thereby saving his country, shows the importance of keeping the protective system in good shape.

Save Some Land, Lose Some Land

While an estimated 2,745 square miles (7,109 sq km) of land were reclaimed from the sea by the Netherlands between 1200 and 1970, about 2,000 square miles (5,180 sq km) were lost to erosion by ocean waves.

The Oosterschelde barrier is the last component of the dams, dikes, and storm barriers of the Delta Project.

Dealing with Nature

In the 1960s and 1970s, the Netherlands started the Delta Project. Dams, dikes, and storm barriers were constructed and the shoreline was shortened by 435 miles (700 km). A 3.5-mile (5.8-km) bridge, one of the longest in Europe, was built across the eastern Schelde River in 1965. The sprawling Rotterdam harbor, the Europoort, was expanded. In 1967, an existing deep channel was extended from the North Sea to Amsterdam.

The Netherlands has few natural resources other than the extensive gas fields near Groningen. Some oil was found near The Hague and in the northeast corner of the country in the 1960s, but the Netherlands still imports most of its petroleum. Coal mines in the vicinity of Limburg were once important to the economy but they have long since been used up. The provinces of Overijssel and Groningen still have working salt mines.

Environmental Challenges

Pollution is one the biggest challenges facing the Netherlands today. The country actively works on the international scene to protect water and air. A Blue Flag award is given to coastal communities that make special efforts to keep their beaches and marinas clean.

Every seven years, the Dutch survey the quantities of nonhazardous waste created by mining, manufacturing, construction, and public utilities. The data are obtained through written questionnaires from 10,000 Dutch businesses with ten or more employees. The results are studied so that the Netherlands can better monitor and cut pollution. In 1994, these firms generated 9.1 million tons of waste, of which 46 percent was recycled.

To preserve their countryside, some Dutch citizens wish to halt land reclamation and delay the construction of more dikes. They feel that land reclamation upsets the natural ecology, and that enough land has been taken back from the sea.

New windmills are used for energy production.

Looking at the Netherlands' Cities

Rotterdam was chartered in 1328. It is the world's largest seaport and the principal center of overseas trade for the Netherlands. It is located 18 miles (29 km) inland on the Rhine (Waal) River. Famous landmarks include the Boymans-van Beuningen Museum (1847) and Erasmus University of Rotterdam (1973). Almost 600,000 people live in Rotterdam. Its average daily temperature is 50°F (10°C).

The Hague is the seat of government for the Netherlands, and the capital of the province of South Holland. It is the site of the International Court of Justice and Europol. Places to visit are the Binnenhof (Inner Court) and Buitenhof (Outer Court), a group of government structures dating in part from the thirteenth century. These buildings include the Palace of the States-General, the Courts of Justice, and the Ridderzaal (Hall of the Knights). The Peace Palace (1913), home of the International Court of Justice, is also located in The Hague. About 440,000 people live here. The average daily temperature is 50°F (10°C).

CHAPTER

THREE

Flatlands, Flowers, and Creatures

W OODLANDS AND FORESTS ARE IMPORTANT TO THE DUTCH. Across the Netherlands, great stands of silver and giant fir, china jute, maples, box elders, and horse chestnuts dot the countryside. Leafy sycamores and delicate alders shade wide city streets and expansive parks feature beautiful roses.

Planting of the Amsterdamse Forest began in 1934, providing work for 20,000 people during the Great Depression when the world's economy collapsed. The last tree in the forest was planted in 1970. The forest has 125 miles (201 km) of hiking trails, 32 miles (51 km) of cycle paths, and fifty bridges.

The Bos, one of the largest parks in Europe, covers 2,148 acres (869 ha) and its 150 varieties of trees are home to about 200 bird species. A monument in the park is dedicated to the victims of Nazi concentration camps in World War II.

Green Areas Planted

To slow erosion by the wind, plots of evergreens have been planted over about 7 percent of the countryside. Dutch forestry workers carefully tend to

Opposite: **The Keukenhof Gardens in Lisse**

The Dutch beautify their country with rows of trees and flowers.

their leafy charges. The Society for Environmental Conservation and the Netherlands Foundation for International Nature Protection make sure everyone does their job well.

The Dutch point to Amsterdam as an example of the greenery of their cities. There are more than 200,000 trees in Amsterdam's open spaces. As long ago as 1454, it was a crime to damage any tree in the town. Laws have been enforced since 1615 to protect the gardens of twenty-seven residential blocks surrounded by canals. A homeowner needs a permit to cut down a tree. But first, a study has to be done on how it will affect the neighborhood. The city even has a government official in charge of environmental issues.

Amsterdam built its first park, the Plantage, in 1682. Today, the city has twenty-eight parks.

Plenty of Flowers

Hortus Botanicus, Amsterdam's main botanical garden, has 6,000 plant species from all climatic zones. An herb garden there dates from 1683. The collection includes descendants of East African coffee plants brought to the Netherlands by the Dutch East India Company in the seventeenth century. The first coffee bush was planted in 1706. Descendants of this plant were sent to start plantations in Brazil, now one of the world's leading coffee suppliers.

Many types of lush vegetation grow well in the Netherlands' rich, spongy soil. Yarrow, wolf's bane, sneezewort, maidenhair fern, hedge garlic, wild onions, bog rosemary, and marsh foxtail can be found by any sharp-eyed hiker carrying a field guide to wild plants.

Queen of the Flowers

The tulip is of course the queen of flowers in the Netherlands. Using advanced techniques, horticulturists (flower growers) get extremely high yields. The tulip's delicate shape, delightful scent, and brilliant colors contribute to its worldwide popularity. Tulips bloom mostly from the end of March to the end of May. In April, when the blossoms are fully opened, an annual celebration of flowers stretches from Noordwijk to Haarlem. A colorful procession of floats wends its way through all the towns along the route. During this season, flower lovers enjoy visiting the Keukenhof, the country's major bulb park near Lisse. The 70-acre (28-hectare) grounds have almost 7 million flowering bulbs amid the pathways, fountains, and ponds.

Maidenhair fern

Tulip Mania

Tulips were first brought to the Netherlands in 1593 when botanist Carolus Clusius planted bulbs imported from Turkey in the Botanical Garden of Leiden. Within a few years, the tulips had become very valuable. By 1620, investors were using gold to pay for premium tulip bulbs. This demand forced the prices to climb steadily for another sixteen years until the market finally collapsed. The collapse of the tulip market brought financial ruin to many Dutch businesspeople. Today, the Dutch export 6.5 billion bulbs worldwide each year. Every spring, more than a million tourists come to the Netherlands to see the tulips in bloom.

Animal Homeland

Many species of animals live in the Netherlands. However, the country's landscape has been altered in many ways over the centuries. Any open, dry land is cultivated or is part of an urban zone. Approximately 65 percent of the Netherlands is used for farming. There are few large areas of natural vegetation but dune grasses and heather on the remaining bog lands provide a safe haven for rabbits. However, larger animals are found only in protected parks or zoos today.

Rare red deer and wild boar live in the forests of Hoge Veluwe National Park near Arnhem in Gelderland. Both animals were once hunted by the nobility and are now protected species. On a sunny afternoon, it is fun to stroll through the grounds of the Royal Rotterdam Zoo or watch the animals playing at the Burger's Zoo in Arnhem. Amsterdam's Artis Zoological Garden, founded in 1838, is the oldest in Europe. Since 1992, Artis has managed an endangered species program for the more than 200 members of the European Association of Zoos and Aquaria.

Exotic, endangered animals such as the rare blackfooted penguin also comfortably loll about in the country's zoos, which are noted for their preservation efforts. The Artis breeds many ancient varieties of farm animals to ensure their future. Among them are blackface sheep, crested ducks, and various types of cows, pigs, and goats.

The red deer is now a protected species.

A cattle egret

Migratory Birds Monitored

As land was reclaimed from the sea, new habitats for many species of migratory birds were formed. These flocks augment the local birds who quack, chatter, and peep along the waterways, in the linden trees, and across pasturelands. Many city dwellers keep homing pigeons in cages on their roofs. To keep track of its wild-bird population, the country has had an official census since the 1970s. Over the years, information gathered in the bird count has helped the country protect its numerous resident and visiting species. The Netherlands Society for the Protection of Birds works hard to ensure that habitats are preserved for future generations.

Information on breeding habits and migration helped with the adoption of a national nature policy plan in 1990. Since birds pay no attention to political borders, the scientific study accompanying the census is done with the support of the European Bird Census. The Dutch are also active participants in international conferences on birds. They even have a Dutch bird page on the Internet.

Bird counts have kept track of the red-throated dive, little grebe, great shearwater, storm petrel, cattle egret, purple heron, black stork, and mute swan, among numerous others. Just think of the varieties of goose that call the Netherlands their home: the pink-footed, the white-fronted, the lesser white-fronted, the gray-lag, the snow, the Canada, the bar-headed, the barnacle, the brent, the pale-bellied brent, the red-breasted, and the Egyptian, to mention just a few. The Dutch laugh at all this, saying the only goose that is missing is the one that lays the golden eggs.

A purple heron

Creepy Crawlies

Several Dutch organizations monitor reptiles living in the Netherlands. Since the early 1990s, the researchers have collected data on the grass snake, the sand lizard, and other creepy, crawly critters that are important in balancing the country's ecosystem. Among its amphibian families, the Netherlands also counts the smooth newt, the tree frog, the natterjack toad, the spotted salamander, and the yellow-bellied toad.

The natterjack toad

Looking Back

I MAGINE THE NETHERLANDS THOUSANDS OF YEARS AGO: It is a raw, blustery day, dampened by a heavy mist. Waves roar against the low sand dunes and shorebirds screech into the wind. Shivering in their animal-skin cloaks, men and women slosh through ankle-deep marsh water. Hungry and tired, they seek a dry place to settle in for the night. Finally finding a mound of grass, they curl up in the gathering darkness to sleep. By dawn the next day, they are gone.

Traces of their passing, such as bone-chip tools, have been found by archaeologists. However, the frosty Ice Age blocked any permanent settlement of the wet Netherlands for centuries. It wasn't until about 4500–4000 B.C. that people from central Europe moved in and built the first primitive villages. Over the next thousand years or so, they were joined by other wandering bands.

Warlike Tribes Move In

About 300 B.C., the warlike Germanic Teutons and Celts muscled into the region that is now the Netherlands, Luxembourg, and Belgium—known as the Low Countries because of their low-lying geography. The

Opposite: **Philip III the Good, Duke of Burgundy by Roger Van der Weyden**

Portrait of a West Friesian Couple with Their Two Children by Mijnerts Herman Doncker

Teutons primarily went to the north and the Celts to the south. The cattle-breeding Frisians, who were a branch of the Teutons, occupied most of today's Netherlands. Over the next few hundred years, the Frisians and other Teutonic clans expanded their hold on the land. By the first century B.C., they had pushed the Celts across the North Sea to what is now Britain. In this era, much of Western Europe fell under the control of the Romans, who supported their Teuton allies in their expansion.

The Franks, another Germanic tribe, were the next major group to move into this area. Settling on the banks of the River Rhine, the Franks soon became the dominant tribe. Their dialect, called *Franconian*, is the core of the modern Dutch language. The Frankish empire eventually grew to be the strongest in Europe in those days.

Frisians Move West

Faced with ever-growing Frankish power, the Frisians moved farther west to settle the seashore and coastal islands. After a long struggle, Christian monks converted many of them. The Frisians became great traders by the A.D. 700s, sending their merchant ships as far away as the Baltic Sea. Their wealthy settlements attracted the attention of the Vikings, who were looting and burning their way through Western Europe. These pagan Scandinavians rowed southward in their low, sleek longboats, pouring out of what are now Norway, Sweden, and Denmark. In their search for treasure, they roamed far afield. Returning with slaves and stolen treasure, they paused in the

Netherlands. Some stayed and settled in, adding another drop to the makeup of today's Dutch people.

A Norse Raid under Olaf

Area United

The Frankish emperor Charlemagne was able to politically unite the area for a time, but when he died in 814 A.D., his empire fell apart. It split into an eastern wing, which later became Germany, and a western kingdom that would become France. The Low Countries were divided between the two, with the Netherlands becoming part of the eastern kingdom called Lorraine.

Through the 1100s, as the first dikes were built and commercial interests expanded, a merchant class developed, and

Bust of Charlemagne in gold and silver

towns grew. The richest cities organized the Hanseatic League, a far-flung economic federation that provided security from pirates and offered trading benefits to its members.

Europe was constantly in turmoil as early nation-states juggled for territory in the 1300s. Several nobles in the region became very powerful, but the French dukes of Burgundy were the cleverest. They used a mix of war, intermarriage, and land purchase to take over most of the Low Countries. Notions of a strong central government took root, especially among the business leaders who needed peace to promote trade. Local assemblies were organized, with merchants, nobles, churchmen, and large landowners participating. During the rule of Philip the Good in the mid-1400s, representatives of these assemblies first came together to discuss mutual interests. This marked the birth of the States-General, which eventually evolved into today's modern Dutch parliament.

Political Maneuvering

All this time, there was great maneuvering on the part of Europe's nobility. Everyone wanted a piece of the political and economic action. Mary of Burgundy, Philip's granddaughter, was married to Archduke Maximilian of the Hapsburgs in 1477, linking the Low Countries to the Hapsburgs' growing empire. In 1516, their grandson Charles I inherited the kingdom of Spain, which put the Low Countries under Spanish control. In 1519, Charles was named archduke of Austria. He eventually became Holy Roman Emperor Charles V. He appointed *stadtholders*, local political leaders, to govern the provinces of what are now the Netherlands and Belgium.

The people of the Netherlands were Roman Catholics at this time. However, Europe was in turmoil as dissenters tried to get the Catholic Church to change its ways. Bishops and other leaders of the Church often acted more like politicians or merchants than religious leaders. Criticism of the Church led to the Protestant Reformation and reformist ideas flashed across the Netherlands' spiritual landscape in the 1500s, attracting many followers. A nervous Church, propped up by Charles's military might, rejected the reforms and persecuted John Calvin and other Protestants. An aging Charles gave up his throne in 1555, but his legacy was carried on by his son, Philip II of Spain, who snatched up the reins of power.

Philip did not understand the importance of independence and freethinking to the Dutch. He increased the religious and political persecution, raised taxes for his wars, and stationed Spanish troops in Dutch towns. Thousands of Dutch reformers fled the country.

Outraged by Philip's conduct, William of Orange and other Dutch nobles rebelled in 1568. As Spanish troops occupied their cities and wheat prices rose, the Dutch people supported the revolt. William and his allies called themselves the Sea Beggars and attacked Spanish ships, spreading panic along the European coast. By 1572, they had captured the provinces of Zeeland and Holland.

William of Orange Leads the Way

William of Orange was born in 1533 and inherited the princedom of Orange in France. Although nicknamed William the Silent because of his cautious nature, he learned to speak excellent French. Educated in the court of Charles V, he was widely admired for his military skill. Although he was raised a Catholic and was a Lutheran for a time, he eventually became a Calvinist.

William led the Dutch revolt against the Spanish and founded the Dutch Republic. He was murdered in 1584 in Delft, the Netherlands. King Philip of Spain put a price on his head and William of Orange was killed by an insane assassin.

Fighting a Common Enemy

Though they still had their differences, Protestants in the north and Catholics in the south of the Netherlands joined forces to fight the invaders. Realizing it was best to unite against a common enemy, representatives of the provinces signed the Pacification of Ghent in 1576. This important document firmly established freedom of religion in the Netherlands, making it a haven for dissenters of all kinds. The next year, they signed the Union of Brussels, which politically united the provinces.

In 1577, the provinces voted to reject the Spanish governor unless Philip pulled out his troops and agreed to Dutch demands for religious freedom. The king agreed to the terms and an uneasy peace reigned.

Independent Political Traditions

Unity did not last long among the Dutch provinces, however. The three southern provinces, which later became Belgium, were staunchly Catholic. They declared their loyalty to the Spanish king in 1579. In the same year, the seven northern provinces of Friesland, Overijssel, Utrecht, Zeeland, Gelderland, Groningen, and Holland formed their own union. They signed the Union of Utrecht in 1581, declaring themselves the United Provinces of the Netherlands. This "nation" did not have a king as ruler, but named William of Orange as a civilian administrator. Establishing this model of government was another important step in developing today's Dutch political system.

Spain did not recognize the United Provinces and attacked again. The resulting war lasted from 1579 to 1609. This drain on money and manpower hurt Dutch trade, especially after the Spanish captured Portugal, a Dutch trading partner in Southeast Asia. Dutch merchants went on to establish the Dutch East India Company, however, which was empowered by the government to make treaties with foreign rulers. The company acquired Southeast Asian colonies for the Netherlands in the seventeenth century.

The Peace of Westphalia's Treaty of Muenster

The Peace of Westphalia was signed in 1648, ending long years of war. Under its terms, the Spanish king finally recognized the Netherlands as a free country. Spain also gave the Dutch its colonies in the Caribbean. This ushered in

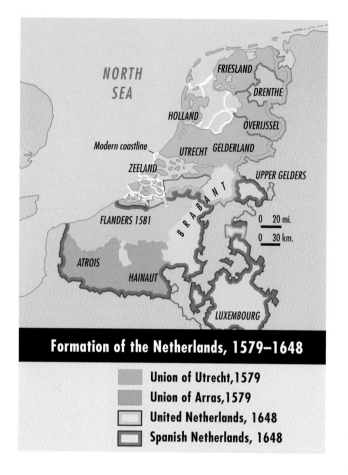

NORTH SEA

FRIESLAND

DRENTHE

HOLLAND

OVERIJSSEL

Modern coastline

UTRECHT GELDERLAND

ZEELAND

UPPER GELDERS

B R A B A N T

FLANDERS 1581

0   20 mi.

0   30 km.

ATROIS

HAINAUT

LUXEMBOURG

Formation of the Netherlands, 1579–1648

Union of Utrecht, 1579
Union of Arras, 1579
United Netherlands, 1648
Spanish Netherlands, 1648

a Golden Age of commerce and the arts for the Netherlands. Amsterdam became Europe's business capital as the Dutch made their economic mark on the world.

Trouble Looms

Yet trouble loomed. The House of Orange and merchants known as Republicans disagreed on religious and business issues. Led by Johan de Witt, the Republicans were concerned that the House of Orange wanted to put a monarch in power. They effectively blocked these efforts, but a mob killed De Witt when Dutch armies under his leadership were defeated by the French. The States-General then made William III, prince of Orange, a *stadtholder*, or governor. He was able to push back the French and regained the country's lost lands.

Because William's wife, Mary, was heir to the English throne, William and Mary also became joint rulers of England in 1689. After more successful battles against the French, William died without an heir in 1702. Without a strong ruler, the Netherlands was largely ignored in the ensuing peace talks.

Throughout the eighteenth century, Dutch economic and political power declined. Then, in the early 1800s, the French emperor Napoleon Bonaparte cast his eye over Europe. His

Microscopic Vision

Dutch scientist Anton van Leeuwenhoek was born in Delft in 1632. At the age of sixteen, while working in a fabric shop, he used a magnifying glass to find rips and tears in the cloth. He then used this experience to grind better lenses and eventually made one of the first microscopes. Eager to learn more, he examined bugs, film from his teeth, blood corpuscles, fish scales, and even bacteria. His writings on the subject earned him the title "Father of Microbiology." He died in 1723.

armies were marching everywhere, expanding French-controlled territory. In 1806, Napoleon claimed the Netherlands as part of his kingdom and installed his brother Louis as king. Much to everyone's surprise, Louis supported the Dutch. For this reason, he was removed from the throne in 1810, and the Netherlands was absorbed into the French Empire.

A Constitutional Monarchy

Napoleon's defeats on the European battlefield over the next few years weakened his political position. Dutch leaders felt the time was right to declare themselves independent again. This time, they set up a constitutional monarchy. The prince of Orange, William V's son, became King William I of the Netherlands.

Belgium and Luxembourg were added to the kingdom's territory by the Congress of Vienna in 1815. Although a period of peace helped the new kingdom, the Belgians wanted out of

the union and rebelled in 1830. William agreed to the division of the kingdom, and Belgium received part of Luxembourg. The remaining part became the Grand Duchy of Luxembourg, which recognized William as its grand duke.

Subsequent kings worked hard to improve the lives of the Dutch people. Canals were dug, dikes were improved, and economic reforms were put into place. When King William III died in 1890, he was succeeded by his daughter, ten-year-old Wilhelmina. While the Netherlands allowed women to become monarchs, Luxembourg did not. As a result, the grand duchy ended its alliance with the Netherlands and became an independent country. For the first few years of her long reign, Wilhelmina's mother was a regent, a person who acts as ruler.

State portrait of Queen Wilhelmina wearing her crown

Rule by a Wise Queen

Wilhelmina was a wise and just queen. She kept the Netherlands neutral during World War I (1914–1918), and led the country through numerous political reforms after the war. Labor insurance, extended voting rights, and better working conditions were happily received by the Dutch. The people were hard hit, however, by the Great Depression. This worldwide economic disaster affected rich and poor alike—banks closed, businesses collapsed, and many people lost their jobs and their homes.

During this difficult time, some European countries were taken over by dictators. Adolf Hitler and his Nazi Party gained power in Germany, the Netherlands' eastern neighbor. Seeking a way out of their own financial woes, some Dutch people supported Hitler's ideas.

World War II

Hitler's armies took over several European countries in the late 1930s. The Netherlands wanted to be neutral but those hopes were dashed when Germany invaded the country on May 10, 1940. Rotterdam was destroyed by bombs and many civilians died. Queen Wilhelmina escaped to Britain. The war took a terrible toll on the Dutch, who tried to resist in many ways. They could be arrested for any reason. Some boys even spent months in jail for playing soccer with a German officer's cap they had found.

Children waiting to be released from Auschwitz concentration camp in 1945

The Anne Frank House is now an important museum in Amsterdam.

Almost every Jewish person in the Netherlands was sent to a death camp, despite the efforts of many Dutch people to protect their neighbors. One of the most poignant museums in Amsterdam is the home in which Anne Frank was hidden from the Nazis during that terrible war. In a now-famous diary, the young Jewish girl wrote about her life and times. She and her family lived in the attic of a small brick house on Prinsengracht until 1944, when they were finally captured and put to death in a concentration camp. The war ended with the defeat of the Nazis, but the Netherlands was in ruins.

Foreign Aid

Foreign aid helped the Dutch begin to rebuild their country. They also joined the new United Nations and the North Atlantic Treaty Organization. In 1949, the Netherlands was faced with growing demands for independence from its Southeast Asian colonies. Still weak from the effects of the war, the Netherlands released its hold on Sumatra, Java, Borneo, and Sulawesi. This vast spread of islands became the nation of Indonesia.

A New Era

Because of her failing health, Queen Wilhemina stepped down from the throne in 1948. When she abdicated, her daughter Juliana became queen. Juliana led the Netherlands into a new era of prosperity. An economic coalition was formed with Belgium and Luxembourg in 1948 and strengthened in 1960.

Sweeping Changes

The 1960s were turbulent times in the Netherlands as young Dutch people made their voices heard, much like their contemporaries in other Western countries. Their intense political activity took an older generation of leaders by surprise. Legislative reforms were enacted when young lawmakers showed that the queen's husband had taken money for helping an American airplane manufacturer in 1976. Deep changes in Dutch society were reflected in the rising divorce rate and the use of drugs.

On the international front, the Netherlands granted independence in 1975 to its South American colony of Suriname. This resulted in a flood of refugees to the Netherlands, adding another ethnic ingredient to the cultural stew. The new arrivals feared that a civil war would break out in the former colony between various political, religious, and ethnic factions. That threat, however, never materialized.

Queen Juliana ended her reign in April 1980. Her daughter, Beatrix, was then installed as monarch. Beatrix ably led her country through the 1990s and on into the next century.

Socialists in The Hague went on a hunger strike in front of the U.S. embassy in 1966 to protest the war in Vietnam.

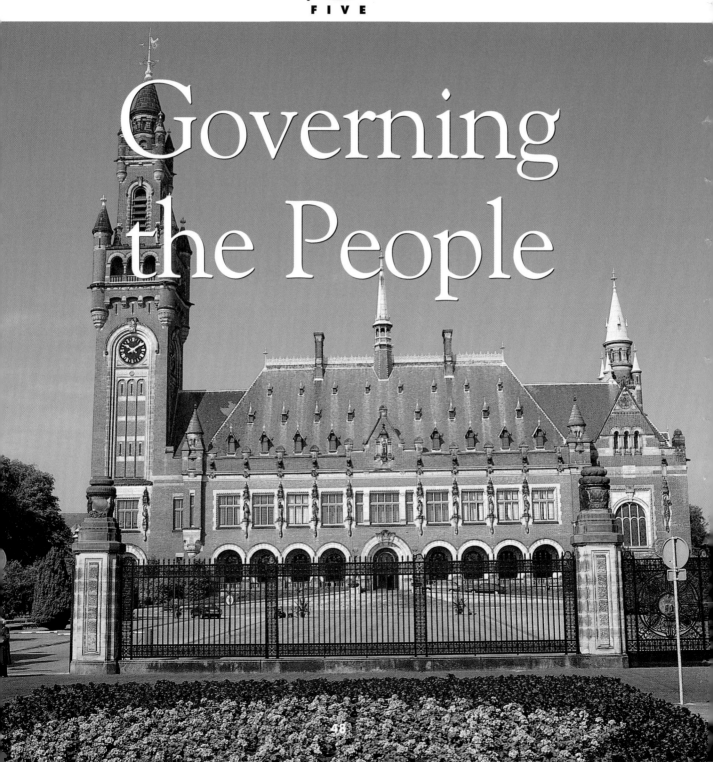

Governing the People

T HE NETHERLANDS IS PART OF THE KINGDOM OF THE Netherlands. The kingdom consists of the mainland nation and the Caribbean islands of Aruba and the Netherlands Antilles—two groups of islands. Although the Netherlands is a monarchy, with a king or queen as symbolic head of state, it has a democratic government with elected leaders and a Constitution.

The Constitution of the Netherlands was written in 1814. The document, revised often to keep up with the times, spells out the rights and responsibilities of the people. The Constitution was most recently updated in 1983.

A prime minister is responsible for running the Netherlands' day-to-day affairs. The prime minister selects members of the Cabinet and the Cabinet decides government policy.

Cabinet members are in charge of governmental departments. The minister of finance is the second-most-powerful figure in the cabinet. The prime minister and secretaries cannot belong to parliament, sit on the Supreme Court or the General

Opposite: **Peace Palace, headquarters for the International Court of Justice, The Hague**

Government buildings in Curacao, Netherlands Antilles

Amsterdam Royal Palace

Auditing Court, or serve on the Council of State. When issues arise in the Cabinet about the Dutch island colonies, their ministers take part in the discussions.

Parliamentary Government

The Netherlands' parliament is called the States-General. It consists of two houses. The 75 members of the First Chamber are elected to four-year terms by the legislatures of the provinces. The Second Chamber has 150 members, elected by the voters for four-year terms.

The Dutch system gives each political party a share of seats on the Second Chamber, depending on the number of votes cast for them. Since World War II ended in 1945, no single party has held a majority of seats in the Second Chamber so coalition or "partnership" governments have been formed. In the Netherlands, only the Second Chamber of the States-General and the monarch, through the Cabinet, can propose legislation. Bills must then be approved by both chambers.

The Dutch parliament meets in The Hague's beautiful Binnenhof. The Binnenhof was the principal court of the counts of Holland in the 1300s. Many buildings surrounding the Binnenhof hold the offices of governmental departments.

At the beginning of a parliamentary session, usually the third Tuesday in September, the monarch rides in a golden coach to the Binnenhof to formally open a joint meeting of both chambers. The queen gives a speech and talks about the country's budget, much as the U.S. president makes a State of the Union address. The two chambers hold joint sessions at the end of a parliamentary session, for the inauguration of a monarch, or for a declaration of war.

The Hague's Binnenhof, the meeting place of the Dutch parliament

The Monarchy

The royal house was founded by William of Orange (1533–1584). Succession in the Dutch monarchy is by *primogeniture*. This means that the first-born child of the royal family is the heir to the throne, whether the child is male or female.

Beatrix (right) became queen in 1980. Queen Beatrix is married to Prince Claus of Germany and their three sons are Willem-Alexander (born 1967), Johan-Friso (1968), and Constantijn (1969). Prince Willem will succeed his mother as monarch.

An Early Feminist

Dutch feminist Etta Lubina Johanna Palm was born in 1743. In an era when women were supposed to be quiet and stay at home, Palm was a strong advocate of women's right to vote and the education of girls. In 1792, Palm gave a famous speech to the French Legislative Assembly in which she outlined her issues.

Monarch as Head of State

The king or queen is the head of state in the Netherlands, but the monarch's duties are largely ceremonial. The monarch co-signs legislation passed by parliament and appoints government officials.

Unlike the monarchy in other countries, Dutch royalty is not crowned. Instead, a ceremony called *investiture* emphasizes that power is given to the monarch by the people. This tradition extends back to the Middle Ages, when new rulers asked towns to swear allegiance to them. In return, the nobility promised to protect the rights of the townspeople.

Remember the stadtholders—the local political leaders of the States of Holland in the fourteenth century? None of the various stadtholders was another's servant, nor his master. Instead, they depended on one another. As an example, when the States of Holland first united under stadtholder William of

Palace guards

Orange, he commanded the army and the stadtholders paid the bills. The early Dutch considered this powerful stadtholder to be a king without the name. In fact, William was the founder of the royal family that rules the Netherlands today.

Investiture of the monarch takes place in Amsterdam, the official capital of the Netherlands. Unlike other nations, another city, The Hague, is the Netherlands' seat of government. All government offices are located in The Hague. The city's official name is *Gravenhage*, but it is generally shortened in Dutch to *Den Haag*.

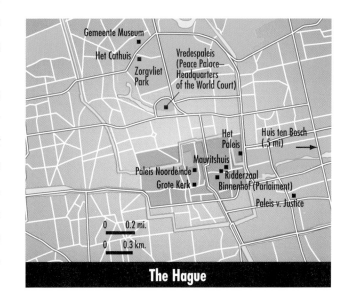

The Hague

GOVERNMENT OF THE NETHERLANDS

Monarch

Council of State
(up to 28 members)

Court of Audit
(3 members)

Administrative

Prime Minister

Cabinet
(14 members)

Legislative

The States-General
(Parliament)

First Chamber
(75 Members)

Second Chamber
(150 Members)

Judicial

Supreme Court

Courts of Appeal

District Courts

Subdistrict Courts

Royal Appointments

The Council of State is presided over by the monarch. Its twenty royal appointees and a vice president advise the king or queen on what is happening in the country. From these discussions, the monarch can issue a royal decree, which is countersigned by a Cabinet minister. The heir to the throne becomes a member of the Council at age eighteen.

The three members of the Court of Audit are appointed for life by the monarchy, based on nominations by the Cabinet. The Court oversees government expenditures and reports to the monarch and the parliament.

Political Parties and Representation

In the 1990s, the leftist Democrats 66 and the Labor Party were among the Netherlands' major parties. A liberal centrist party, the Christian Democratic Appeal, was also popular. There were also numerous smaller parties, ranging from the radical left to the very conservative and those with a labor or religious bent.

An Agent for Change

Pieter Jelles Troelstra (1860–1930) was one of the Netherlands' most powerful politicians. He formed the Social Democratic Labor Party and was a leader in the country's November Revolution of 1918. He supported an eight-hour workday and the right of women to vote and run for national office. Troelstra also advocated abolition of the monarchy. By the time he died, all the causes he championed had been put into effect, except the abolition of royalty.

A resident casts his vote in the general elections at a voting booth set up inside a family home.

Some political parties advocate environmental issues; others concentrate on social causes. Everyone in the Netherlands seems to have a point of view and up to twenty-five parties sometimes take part in an election. This reaffirms that the people have a wide spectrum of opinions. This has been a traditional part of the Dutch heritage.

Workers and their bosses are equally represented on a government-mandated Economic and Social Council and a Joint Industrial Labor Council. These organizations help the government plan its economic policy.

Voter Responsibilities

Usually, everyone in the Cabinet supports a similar platform—a set of goals and ideas. But sometimes the prime minister, the cabinet, and the parliament cannot agree. The Cabinet then resigns or parliament is dissolved, and elections take place. Dutch citizens aged 18 and older vote for their representatives.

Prior to 1970, all citizens were required by law to vote. Although voting is no longer compulsory, the Dutch take this responsibility seriously. More than 80 percent of eligible voters turn out for elections. In comparison, usually no more than 50 percent of the voters take part in national elections in the United States, and 50 to 60 percent vote in Canada, depending on the issues. Elections in the Netherlands are held every four years in May, unless parliament is dissolved early.

This republican philosophy, where the supreme power of the nation rests with the voters and is exercised by elected representatives, has long been a tradition in the Netherlands.

The National Flag

The flag of the Netherlands has three equal horizontal bands of red, white, and blue. Dating from around 1630, it is based on a flag flown by the House of Orange. After 1630, the red band gradually replaced the original orange band.

The Legal System

The Dutch legal system is a mixture of Roman and Napoleonic civil law. There are no jury trials in the Netherlands. Minor cases are heard by single judges, while tribunals of several justices oversee important cases.

The Supreme Court, consisting of twenty-four to twenty-six justices, is the Netherlands' highest court. The monarch names all its justices, who are appointed for life though most retire at age seventy.

The Supreme Court does not review cases, as in the United States, but ensures that there has been a uniform application of the law and that all procedures were correctly followed. The Supreme Court cannot declare a law unconstitutional. Only the monarch and the States-General (parliament) have that authority.

In addition to the Supreme Court, there are sixty-one subdistrict courts, nineteen district courts, and five courts of appeal. There is also a juvenile court for troubled youngsters between twelve and seventeen. In 1982, the office of a national investigator was established by the Second Chamber. This *ombudsman*, appointed for a six-year term, resolves disputes between Dutch citizens and the government.

The National Anthem

The Dutch national anthem is *Wilhelmus van Nassouwe* ("William of Nassau"). It was written around 1568, possibly by the poet and diplomat Philip van Marnix, Seigneur of Sint Aldegonde (1538–1598). It has been the official national anthem since 1932.

The song has fifteen verses, but usually only the first and sixth verses are sung at national events. In the first verse, Prince William promises that he will remain true to his country even if he dies. In the sixth verse, he prays for strength to rid the Netherlands of tyranny.

Verse 1

William of Nassau, scion
Of a Dutch and ancient line,
I dedicate undying
Faith to this land of mine.
A prince I am, undaunted,
Of Orange, ever free,
To the king of Spain I've granted
A lifelong loyalty.

Verse 6

A shield and my reliance,
O God, Thou ever wert.
I'll trust unto Thy guidance.
O leave me not ungirt.
That I may stay a pious
Servant of Thine for aye
And drive the plagues that try us
And tyranny away.

City Hall, Rotterdam

Local Government

The Netherlands is made up of twelve provinces: Drenthe, Flevoland, Friesland, Gelderland, Groningen, Limburg, Noord-Brabant, Noord-Holland, Overijssel, Utrecht, Zeeland, and Zuid-Holland. These provinces are similar to states in the United States and provinces in Canada.

Each province is governed by a commissioner and a council. The commissioner is appointed by the monarch, and the council is elected by the people. The number of council representatives depends on the number of citizens in the province.

The Netherlands has about 850 cities and towns. Each has an elected council and a *burgomaster* appointed by the monarch.

Military Responsibility

In keeping with their long military history, the Dutch armed forces are highly trained. Branches of the volunteer service include the Royal Netherlands Army, Royal Netherlands Navy (including a naval air and marine corps), Royal Netherlands Air Force, and Royal Constabulary.

The Dutch have provided troops for United Nations (UN) peace-keeping actions, and Dutch troops served with distinction during the Korean War in the 1950s. They have also been on the front lines in the Middle East, Africa, and Bosnia. The

Netherlands is a member of the North Atlantic Treaty Organization (NATO) and regional security groups.

In the 1970s, men and women in the services campaigned strenuously for more individual rights. The secretary of defense dropped the requirement that soldiers in uniform salute superior officers. Long hair and beards also were allowed. Of course, none of this has affected the fighting capabilities of the Dutch. The Dutch military readily survived all these challenges.

Work for Peace

The International Court of Justice meets regularly in The Hague's Peace Palace. In the late 1800s, Dutch law professor Tobias M. C. Asser (below) was a leading spokesman for world peace. His work resulted in the setting up of a Permanent Court of Arbitration (now the Court of Justice) in The Hague. In 1911, he received the Nobel Peace Prize.

The court is still active. In the late 1990s, the court tried people accused of war crimes in the former Yugoslavia.

Amsterdam: Did You Know This?

Population (1998):	718,175	**Altitude:** 10 feet (3 m)	
Ethnic breakdown (1998):		**Average Daily Temperature:**	
Dutch	405,398	January	36° Fahrenheit (2° C)
Others	132,633	July	62° Fahrenheit (17° C)
Surinamese	70,379	**Average Annual Rainfall:** 34 inches	
Moroccan	50,853	(86 mm)	
Turkish	31,822	**Canals:** more than 50 miles (80 km)	
Southern European	16,372	**Bridges:** Approximately 400	
Antillean	10,718	**Chartered:** 1300	

Economic
Smarts

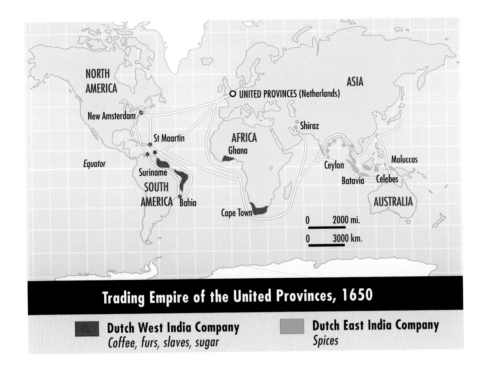

Trading Empire of the United Provinces, 1650

Dutch West India Company
Coffee, furs, slaves, sugar

Dutch East India Company
Spices

S INCE THE FIRST DUTCH TRADING VESSEL SAILED OVER the horizon, the Netherlands has been a business paradise. Its coastal location in Western Europe and waterway connections to the interior of the continent made it an important commercial crossroads. In addition, the Dutch have always had a strong business sense.

This combination of location and "smarts" led to a Golden Age of commerce and culture in the sixteenth century and wealthy merchants formed the Dutch East India Company in 1602. This company had the power to make treaties with

Opposite: **A Frisian cargo boat**

The Secret of Success

In the 1690s, a young Russian visited a Dutch shipyard to learn the secrets of Dutch success. After he returned home, he eventually became known as Czar Peter the Great.

foreign rulers. The Dutch West India Company was established in 1621 and acquired extensive territory in South America. The Netherlands has not rested on its economic laurels. It remains important in the world marketplace.

Dutch traders traveled everywhere. They ventured into North America, the Far East, and South America. Sailors wrote of the hardships on these voyages, but they also described exciting new worlds. Dutch colonies were established from New Amsterdam, which is now New York City, to Jakarta in today's Indonesia. Brazil, several Caribbean islands, and the southern tip of Africa also fell under Dutch control. The powerful Dutch army and navy kept their watchful eyes over this far-flung empire.

A busy seaport in Volendam

Sprawling Seaports

The country's sprawling seaports were noisy, bustling, dirty . . . and always fascinating. People of all social strata, races, colors, and religions jostled their way along the piers and through the warehouses of Rotterdam and Amsterdam.

Storms, pirates, and shipwrecks were always potential disasters. Many heavily laden merchant vessels were lost at sea. Rembrandt's famous portrait *Syndics of the Amsterdam Cloth Guild* shows wealthy businessmen whose ships arrived safely.

Free Enterprise Promotes Economy

Today, the Dutch free-enterprise system is technologically advanced and contributes to a high standard of living in the Netherlands. The Dutch per-capita income—the amount each person earns every year—is among the highest in Europe, and the government wants to keep it that way. It ensures that environmental standards are maintained and keeps a close watch over banking, international trade, and related matters that keep the economy humming. Service industries, such as insurance, marketing, and banking, make up more than 50 percent of the gross national product (GNP). Industry comprises 26 percent of that total, with agriculture at 3 percent.

Office buildings in Rotterdam

The Netherlands exports more than $150 billion in metalwork, chemicals, processed foods, tobacco, and agricultural products to other countries each year. The nation's largest trading partners are Germany, Belgium, Luxembourg, Great Britain, and Eastern Europe.

The country imports about $130 billion in products from other countries each year. Raw materials for its industries, as well as consumer goods, transportation equipment, crude oil, and some food are among its imports. Again, most of this comes from the Netherlands' European partners. Whenever a country imports less than it exports, it is economically successful.

Gross National Product

Gross national product (GNP) is the amount of goods and services a country produces annually. The value of these goods and services during a given period is a measurement of a nation's total economic performance.

European Economic Unity Supported

The Netherlands has always been active in the European Economic Community, now called the European Union (EU). From its original six members, the group of fifteen Western European nations has become the world's largest single market. Its headquarters is in Brussels, Belgium, and it has almost 400 million potential consumers in Europe alone. The Netherlands was a major player in the formation of this economic superpower, which grew out of cooperative trade policies developed in the 1950s and 1960s. Always looking ahead toward ongoing growth and regional stability, the Netherlands joined its partners in calling for a "United Europe" at a summit meeting held in The Hague in 1969.

The Euromast, erected in 1960, allows a view of Rotterdam from 607 feet (185 m) high. It houses an observation deck, a presentation center, and an exclusive restaurant.

In 1990, trade partnerships were made with Canada and the United States. By the early 1990s, the EU's biggest trading partners were the United States, Russia, Japan, China, Central and Eastern Europe, and Scandinavia. The Netherlands, of course, had a slice of that large economic pie.

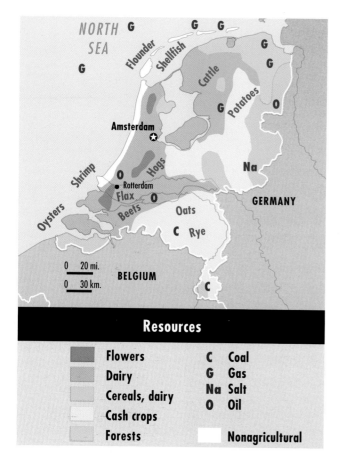

NORTH SEA

Amsterdam

Rotterdam

GERMANY

BELGIUM

0 20 mi.
0 30 km.

Flounder · Shellfish · Cattle · Potatoes · Hogs · Na · Shrimp · Oysters · Flax · Beets · Oats · C Rye · C

Resources

- Flowers
- Dairy
- Cereals, dairy
- Cash crops
- Forests

C Coal
G Gas
Na Salt
O Oil

Nonagricultural

The Netherlands remains active on all levels within this broader European community. In 1992, it proudly hosted the signing of the Maastricht Treaty, which opened up Europe for even more cross-border trade. The treaty also had provisions on security and foreign policy. Money from the EU has helped build bridges, roads, and sports stadiums and has funded arts projects and related activities in the Netherlands and other member countries.

As an economically healthy nation, the Netherlands is also generous. Its foreign-aid program to poorer countries is extensive.

Business Connections Promote Growth

As technology brings the world together, Dutch business leaders take advantage of opportunities that help them expand. They learned their lessons well from their country's commercial history, in which trade partnerships were important. The Dutch often link one of their own industries to an industry in another country.

Royal Dutch Steelworks is a modern example. It was established in 1918 at IJmuiden to give the Netherlands its own source of steel. In 1972, it merged with a German company

Weights and Measures

The Netherlands uses the metric system.

and now ranks among the top steel producers in Europe. Originally a Dutch firm, the parent company of Unilever joined with the British company Lever Brothers in 1929 to make soap and perfume. DAF, an auto firm founded by the son of a blacksmith in 1928, merged in 1974 with Volvo, a Swedish car company.

Of course, some plants remain Dutch-owned. They make wire, steel beams, dock cranes, leather goods, electrical machinery, and barges. Royal Dutch Shell is one of the world's largest chemical manufacturers, as well as an oil refiner. You have probably seen Shell service stations in North America. Firms such as Gassan and Coster Diamonds cut precious gems used in jewelry and industry.

Money Matters

Dutch currency is called the *guilder*—or sometimes the *gulden* or *florin*. In 1999, U.S.$1 was worth 2.07 guilders, and Canadian $1 was worth 1.40 guilders. The guilder is printed in 10, 25, 100, 250, and 1,000 denominations. It is also available as coins worth 1, 2.5, and 5 guilders. Abstract designs of flowers, industrial products, and other objects brighten each note. There are 100 cents in a guilder. The 5-cent coin is called a *stuiver*, the 10-cent coin is known as a *dubbeltje*, and the 25-cent coin is a *kwartje*.

The Dutch have begun using a new form of money called the Euro. Eventually, the Euro will replace the national currencies of most European nations.

Vegetable Growers

Agricultural products from the Netherlands are considered among the best in Europe. In the mid-1990s, the nation ranked third worldwide in the value of its agricultural exports, after the United States and France. Along with more commercial methods of cultivation, some Dutch farmers use organic methods. They cut back on chemical pesticides and artificial fertilizer. About 7 percent of Dutch farmland is now devoted to organic farming.

Rows of greenhouses in Aalsmeer

In the 1970s, the government established national landscape parks to protect the country's historic small farms. Up to 500,000 acres (202,350 ha) were set aside for this purpose, while the nation's remaining 4.4 million acres (1.8 million ha) are more intensively used for agriculture. Wheat, barley, sugar beets, and potatoes are major cash crops. The hothouses that dot the countryside extend the growing season of lettuce, tomatoes, cucumbers, grapes, and flowers.

Cheese for All

Cheese, one of the country's major exports, has been produced in the Netherlands since the Middle Ages. By 1649, the port of Edam was exporting 1 million pounds (0.4 million kg) of cheese a year. Farmers and their families made the cheese and carried it to a weigh-house once a week. The cheese was then shipped to cities such as Alkmaar and Edam for delivery to customers around the world.

Bashing the Cheese

Traditionally, buyers and sellers bartered over the price of cheese. The buyer tested the quality of cheese by "bashing" or hitting it. The cheese was sampled by sticking a borer into the center of the round (large piece of cheese) and pulling out a small piece to determine the flavor.

Workers wearing the colors of their respective companies carried the rounds on "stretchers" to and from the weighing houses. Tourists can see this summer activity re-created at the Alkmaar, Purmerend, and Gouda cheese markets.

Over the centuries, factories gradually took over Dutch cheese production. However, about 600 farms in South Holland and Utrecht still make their own cheese from unpasteurized milk. Cheese lovers claim this cheese is the best.

Fishing Fleets

Dutch fishing fleets catch mackerel, sole, and plaice. Today, the boats have to sail as far as Iceland for a prime catch, due to overfishing in the North Sea. The fishing season opens annually in late May with a festival called Vlaggetjesdag, or Flag Day. This tradition dates back to the fourteenth century. On this day, fishing boats are bedecked with banners and pendants and costumed folk-dancers twirl in time to lively music on the docks and streets of the fishing villages. The biggest celebration is in Scheveningen, near The Hague.

A prize catch is herring, a small fish that has been a staple of the European diet since at least 3000 B.C. Easy to digest, it is a good source of vitamin D, calcium, and minerals that protect the body against disease. Herring is known by different names. *Matjes* are young juicy fish. *Schmaltz*, or fat herring, is less salty than the matjes but is processed with more herbs and spices. Kipper is cold-smoked after pickling. Bismarck herring is marinated in vinegar and salt. All these types of herring are "cured" in a salt bath for varying lengths of time to add flavor.

A herring stall

Yo, Ho, Ho! A-Fishing We Will Go

There are twenty-five large herring boats, each more than 300 feet (91 m) long in the Dutch fishing fleet. Using mechanized equipment, the crew catches, cleans, cures, and freezes the fish. Each captain wants to be the first back to port with his catch of fresh fish. The winner receives a $1,500 prize and then passes it on to Greenpeace, the international environmental organization. Queen Beatrix is traditionally given the year's first barrel of new herring.

The Scots are credited with processing herring in the seventh century. The Dutch became their first customers and quickly grew to love the delicacy. In the fourteenth century, Dutchman Willem Bueckelszoor invented the gibbing process of preparing the fish for market. This process removes the gills and gullet of the fish, taking away any bitter taste. Other organs are left in the fish when it is salted to increase the flavor. For shipment, up to twenty slated herring are packed in a large barrel. Others are packed in smaller containers. Then off they go—to someone's table in Toledo, Toronto, or Tokyo. The herring trade contributed to making the Netherlands an economic powerhouse in the Middle Ages.

Flowers and Visitors

Dutch flower markets carry a variety of flowers and plants.

The Netherlands is flower-mad. Dutch tulips are shipped by the millions to gardeners around the world. Numerous Dutch companies serve all aspects of the floral industry. A company named Blumex exports cut flowers and potted plants while P. Kooij & Zonen B.V. specialize in carnation cuttings. Waterdrinker Aalsmeer is a wholesaler of garden plants and supplies, and Van Staaveren Aalsmeer concentrates on ornamental flowers.

The Netherlands also depends on tourism to support its economy. More than 5 million persons a year visit the country, spending about $2 billion on everything from museum passes, lunches, and taxis to souvenirs. They are attracted to the invigorating art scene, the gentle beauty of the countryside, the wonders of the old cities, and Dutch history.

Canal cruises in Amsterdam are a big attraction for tourists and natives alike.

Easy to Reach

The Netherlands is linked to the world by railroad, highways, airline links, and waterways. Its central location in Europe is very helpful for private and business travel. There are 1,735 miles (2,792 km) of railroad track and 75,078 miles (120,823

A barge carrying containers on the Nieuwe Maas River

km) of paved and gravel roadways. This makes it easy to get goods in and out of the country. High-speed trains also link the Netherlands to the rest of Europe.

Modern Ports

The nation has 3,940 miles (6,340 km) of inland waterways and an extensive system of deep-water harbors that can accommodate heavily laden freighters, barges, or sleek pleasure

craft. Amsterdam, Delfzijl, Dordrecht, Eemshaven, Groningen, Haarlem, Maastricht, Rotterdam, Terneuzen, IJselmuiden, and Utrecht are among the world's most modern ports.

The Dutch are still great sailors. There are more than 400 ships in the Dutch merchant fleet. They include bulk-cargo carriers, oil and gas tankers, refrigerator ships, passenger vessels, and livestock carriers.

Dutch girls dressed in traditional clothes have fun chatting on the phone.

Take a Flight

By air, it is easy to get to the Netherlands, whether you are coming from Saskatoon, San Francisco, or anywhere else. The country has twenty-nine large and small airports. Amsterdam's efficient Schiphol International Airport is the largest, with 10,055 feet (3,065 m) of paved runways and its elaborate, modern terminals. KLM—*Koninklijke Luchtvaart Maatschappij* (Royal Dutch Airlines)—is the national airline of the Netherlands.

The Dutch love to stay in touch with one another. By the end of the 1990s, there were 9,418,000 telephones in the country. There is a nation-wide mobile-phone system and just about everyone in the country seems to have a portable phone stuck to their ear. Three AM and twelve FM radio stations and eight television stations serve an estimated 4.9 million radios and 7.4 million televisions in the Netherlands. In addition to local programming, Dutch broadcasting carries shows from other countries including North America.

The Dutch are also confirmed readers, with forty-five daily newspapers to keep them up to date on politics, sports, culture, and commerce. Amsterdam's *De Telegraf* is the national paper of record. The joke is that if something is not reported in *De Telegraf*, it probably did not happen. There are also newspapers affiliated with religious denominations and political parties.

Union Watchdogs

Organized labor is an important force in the Netherlands. The unions oversee working conditions and wages. There are occasional strikes, but most issues are resolved before such drastic action is needed. Wages are set through government-approved guidelines. In the 1990s, the nation had more jobs than workers. Subsequently, thousands of immigrants came to the Netherlands from Turkey, Greece, and Eastern Europe.

Today, the Dutch people look toward their economic future just as eagerly as their ancestors who set off into uncharted waters. They know it takes hard work to remain economically stable, but that is certainly nothing new for the industrious Dutch.

Many Faces of the Dutch

WITH A POPULATION OF 15,653,091, THE NETHERLANDS is one of Europe's most crowded nations, ranking just behind Monaco and Malta. An average of 1,000 persons live on each square mile (2.6 sq km). Half of the Dutch people reside on the 15 percent of land making up the provinces of North and South Holland.

The Dutch learned long ago to live comfortably with this density, but the housing shortages in some cities make it

Opposite: **A café in Amsterdam**

The Dutch have clever ways of dealing with overpopulation, such as this cube apartment complex in Rotterdam.

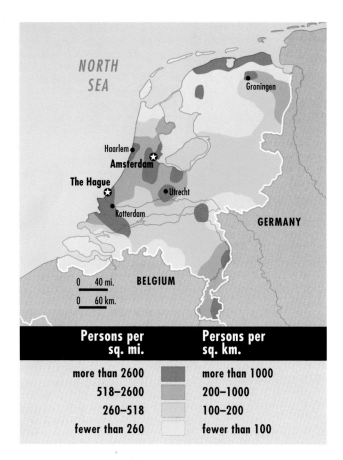

Population distribution of the Netherlands

The Hindu wedding of a Surinamese couple shows the bride veiled in red and the groom in all yellow.

Map legend

Persons per sq. mi.		Persons per sq. km.
more than 2600		more than 1000
518–2600		200–1000
260–518		100–200
fewer than 260		fewer than 100

difficult for young people to have their own homes. New polders created over the past decades ease the space strain. Careful urban planning, excellent transportation services, and old-fashioned concern for one another also help make life easier. In addition, a slight decline in the number of Dutch babies being born in the late 1990s and a slowdown in emigration from other countries also help control growth.

Mixed Heritages

Like many other northern Europeans, most Dutch people have blue eyes, blonde hair, and fair complexions. However, the country has been mixing cultures and physical features for a thousand years. The Dutch are a rainbow of Celt, German, Frankish, Scandinavian Viking, Jewish, French, Indonesian, and Surinamese heritages. More recently, other exotic splashes were added as Turkish and Moroccan workers settled in the Netherlands to raise their families.

Tensions Result

Sometimes the presence of newcomers has caused tension, especially as competition increased for housing and jobs. The Dutch have a long history of accepting new ideas and philosophies by allowing religious and political refugees to live in their country. However, as a people, they often preferred to stay close to their church and local communities. Because the country was so small, it sometimes seemed safer to look inward . . . to themselves.

Population of Major Cities (1997 est.)

Amsterdam	718,175
(1988 est.)	
Rotterdam	599,414
The Hague	440,000
Utrecht	235, 357
Eindhoven	197, 055

Who Lives in the Netherlands?

Dutch:	96%
Moroccan:	1%
Turkish:	1%
Other:	2%

Housing along the Keizers and Leidse Canals in Amsterdam exhibits the close quarters in which many Dutch live.

Traditionally, Dutch society is based on *verzuilung* (customary ways of doing things). Sometimes these ways were called "pillars" holding up society. This resulted from efforts in the nineteenth century to reduce disputes between the country's Roman Catholics and Protestants. Jews had their own social pillars, and nobody cared much for the "neutrals," those Dutch people who didn't attend church and were mostly socialist in their politics. Each of these four groups kept to itself through the 1920s. They had their own publications, soccer clubs, social organizations, and schools.

As life became faster paced and as people traveled extensively outside the Netherlands and learned more about the world, the *verzuilung* system slowly faded out. During both world wars, the Dutch had to break down many of their past barriers and cooperate closely in order to survive as a people. The 1960s brought a big shift in the old way of life too. Throughout the Western world—in Canada, the United States, and other countries—young people were in the forefront of change. They encouraged their elders to think of new ways to overcome political and social challenges. There were protests, marches, and takeovers of universities and government buildings.

The Dutch are politically active. Here, demonstrators protest the decision to deploy U.S. cruise missiles at Woensdrecht NATO base.

A man debates with Amsterdam police outside the headquarters of the squatter movement, which encourages homeless people to occupy abandoned buildings.

It was no different in the Netherlands. As a result, attention was focused on the place of women in society, the environment, antiwar fervor, and the use of drugs. In their plea for more services, homeless squatters occupied abandoned buildings. Intermarriage increased between people of different religions and racial backgrounds. Eventually, the activists graduated from school and moved into positions of influence in government, education, the arts, and social services. They carried their lofty ideals with them, tempered by modern reality.

Two Languages

Common languages help unite a country's citizens. The Netherlands' official language is Dutch, which is used everywhere except in Friesland, where ancient Frisian is spoken.

Street signs in Amsterdam show how common the English language is in Dutch daily life.

Both languages are of Germanic origin. During the Middle Ages, an old form of Dutch called "low German" was spoken in both the Netherlands and northern Germany. Some students of language say that Dutch is a language halfway between English and German.

In Dutch, however, the arrangement of words into sentences is closer to German than English. The words in a Dutch or German sentence fall into different order than they do in an English sentence. For example, read these sentences:

"*Gistern heb ik een man gezien*" (Dutch), and

"*Gestern habe ich einen Mann geshen*" (German).

An English translation would be "Yesterday have I a man seen," while an English speaker would say, "I saw a man yesterday."

Spoken Dialects

There are about twenty-five dialects of Dutch. Flemish is spoken in parts of Belgium. Afrikaans is spoken in South Africa, where there is a large Dutch community. Creole, or pidgin Dutch, a mixture of languages, survives in the former colonies of Suriname and Indonesia. The preferred pronunciation of Dutch is spoken around The Hague, the seat of Dutch government. Slang, used as often in Dutch as in English, changes day to day.

Dutch is taught as a foreign language at universities in many countries, from Poland to Canada to the United States, especially in the upper Midwest, where many Dutch settled. Many societies promote the use of Dutch in the artistic world. The Foundation for the Promotion of the Translation of Dutch Literary Works encourages the English-speaking world to learn more about Dutch authors.

A Common Tongue

In the seventeenth century, scholars encouraged the adoption of standard Dutch. Playwright Joost van den Vondel (1587–1679) and grammar scholar Hendrik Laurenszoon Spieghel (1549–1612) led this effort to find a common tongue.

Frisian came into common usage in the sixteenth century. Originally considered a dialect, Frisian was spoken mostly in the northeastern part of what became the Netherlands. It was recognized as an official language in 1955.

In keeping with the Netherlands' international outlook, almost everyone speaks fluent English. The English language is taught in schools beginning at age 12, making it simple to talk with Dutch youngsters. And English is the basic language used in business. As a result, English words have crept into Dutch usage, as well. Words such as "computer," "jukebox," and "one-man-show" pop up in conversations in the Dutch language.

Common Dutch Words and Phrases

Dutch	Pronunciation	English
ja/nee	ya/nay	yes/no
hallo	hallo	hello
dank u wel	dan oo vel	thank you
als't u blieft	alst oo bleeft	please
kaas	kassa	cheese
Spreekt u engels?	Sprect oo engels?	Do you speak English?
de toilet	toilet	toilet
brood	brood	bread
broodje	brood ja	rolls

Dutch in English

Many phrases in English include the word *Dutch*. For example, you can open the top or the bottom part of a dutch door. A dutch oven is an iron kettle used for baking. When you go dutch treat, you pay your own way to a movie or concert. Dutchman's-breeches are pretty white flowers that bloom in the spring. Dutch words have also found their way into English, with changes in spelling over the years. An artist's *easel*, a frame on which to hang a canvas while it is being painted, was originally an *ezel* (donkey).

Importance of Education

The Dutch literacy rate is 99 percent, which is higher than the 97 percent literacy rate of the United States and Canada. Since 1917, schools in the Netherlands have received public funding. If they wish, parents can send their children to primary school at age four. Otherwise, youngsters must start

Dutch students engaged in school activities

classes by age five and stay in school until they are sixteen. Tests send children into general, preuniversity, or vocational secondary schools.

General secondary schools have junior programs of four years and senior courses of five years. Preuniversity students take six years of classes before applying to an institute of higher learning. Students in vocational schools can learn a trade, such as mechanics or nursing. Summer holidays are staggered so that vacation resorts are not swamped, which might happen if everyone got out of school at once. About one-third of the elementary and secondary schools are public and the remainder are nonpublic, usually affiliated with a church.

About 20 percent of Dutch schoolchildren go on for more advanced studies. There are thirteen universities and fiftynine institutes of higher vocational

The University of Utrecht, established in 1636

training in the Netherlands. They are among Europe's oldest. William of Orange established the University of Leiden in 1575. The University of Groningen was established in 1614, followed by Utrecht in 1636. The government funds all institutes of higher learning and provides interest-free loans to students so that they can afford to attend. Students must do very well in school, however, to get educational loans. Higher learning is so important to the Dutch that many businesspeople put their degrees on their business cards.

Social Services

Different countries provide different levels of help for their citizens. The Dutch feel it is important to take care of one another. Widows, orphans, and families with children get government allowances. The government also provides extensive health and dental insurance for citizens earning less than an annually fixed level. If Dutch citizens lose their jobs, they are entitled to receive up to 75 percent of their previous pay in compensation for a certain amount of time.

Creative Thinking in Health

The Netherlands has an excellent system of health care. As of the late 1990s, average life expectancy was 75 years for men and 81 years for women. Very few Dutch babies die in infancy. As in other developed countries, the leading causes of death among adults are traffic accidents, cancer, and heart problems.

Most hospitals and clinics are privately operated, but medical costs are paid by the government through the national health-insurance program. Home care is available for pregnant women and the elderly. Alternative forms of health care are popular in the Netherlands. Creative therapy can include drama, music, fine arts, and even flower-growing. The Dutch people feel that the combination of a strong body and mind makes the best health team.

With its compact geography and dense population, the Netherlands needs to think creatively about population issues.

A busy day in Amsterdam

As a result, the country often takes the lead in international studies on such questions. The Dutch were proud to host the important European Population Conference held in The Hague in 1999. During the conference, scientists, politicians, educators, and artists previewed trends in living patterns. Their work at the conference will help the world face the next century.

Barriers Break Down

As traditional social barriers break down, so do political boundaries and other barriers that separate people. But on a less positive side, interesting customs may also fall by the wayside when everyone goes "modern." For instance, Dutch people seldom wear their ethnic clothing today. Long ago, men wore dark, baggy pants and shirts and women had color-

Teenagers hanging out on their bikes

ful full dresses, skirts, and bonnets. Today, the average Dutch businessperson wears a suit, and young people hang out in leather jackets, jeans, and T-shirts. Traditions, however, are still celebrated at festivals in the Netherlands and in areas around the world where the Dutch settled. For instance, an annual tulip festival, complete with street-sweeping, garden tours, and dancers wearing wooden shoes is held in Holland, Michigan.

Hearty Fare

The Dutch generally eat much of the same kinds of foods as other Europeans. They have a simple breakfast of cold meat,

Klompen

The Dutch do not wear the clunky wooden shoes called *klompen* much any more. These famous shoes aren't practical for modern city living. Just try walking on hard pavement in wooden shoes! However, farmers and fishers often wear them when the weather is wet because they keep out dampness better than leather boots. Wooden shoes are not worn inside the house because they make too much noise. Most wooden shoes made today are sold to tourists.

cheese, fruit, and bread. Businesspeople eat a light lunch, perhaps a bowl of pea soup with dark rye bread, or *frikandel* (fried sausage). Dinner might consist of meat or fish, with potatoes and vegetables. A popular side dish is raw herring smothered in onions. Pastries such as *oliebollen* (sugar-covered doughnuts) are delicious.

Over the past twenty years, Indonesian cooking has had a great influence on Dutch dishes because Indonesia was a Dutch colony for so long. A delicious meat stew called *hutspot* is popular. *Rijsttafel*, another Indonesian dish, is made up of curried chicken or lamb served with spices, pineapple, and rice. *Nasi goreng*, fried rice with meat and vegetables, and *bambi goreng*, fried noodles, are also tasty treats.

This Indonesian dish consists of tofu, julienne vegetables, and peanut sauce.

The Dutch enjoy eating at restaurants. Some restaurants specialize in huge pancakes topped with berries or other fillings, and *poffertjes* (tiny pancakes). The most inexpensive restaurants are Turkish coffee bars and Surinamese fast-food outlets serving *chicken roti* and other delicacies. Young Dutch people also love going to dance clubs and cafés for late evening fun.

Religious Ways

THE NETHERLANDS HAS ALWAYS BEEN A HAVEN FOR FREE-thinkers, a positive attribute that often got the Dutch in trouble. Other countries sometimes failed to appreciate that the Netherlands harbored their dissenters.

There is no official state religion in the Netherlands where the Constitution emphasizes the separation of church and state. Although the country is considered mostly Protestant, there are actually more Roman Catholics. But the Dutch people who have no religion at all make up the largest group.

About 34 percent of the Netherlanders are Roman Catholics and live in the southern part of the Netherlands. Dutch bishops and cardinals are often quite liberal in their thinking, which sometimes puts them at odds with the Vatican—the seat of authority of the Roman Catholic Church.

Protestants, about 30 percent of the Dutch, live primarily in the north. Among the Protestant groups practicing their faith in the Netherlands are the Dutch Reformed

Opposite: **A traditional Christian church**

Gothic *Nieuwe Kerk*, or New Church, erected 1384–1496 in Delft

Religions of the Netherlands

Roman Catholic	34%
Protestant	30%
Muslim	3%
Other	2%
Unaffiliated	36%

Dutch Come to North America

The first Dutch immigrants came to North America in the early seventeenth century, bringing their religious beliefs with them. At the time of the American Revolution (1775–1783), there were at least 100 Dutch Reformed congregations in the colonies. These groups eventually split to form new congregations throughout the United States and Canada. By the 1840s, there were strong Reformed churches in Michigan and Iowa. The first Canadian Christian Reformed Congregation was formed in 1905 in Alberta.

Church, Mennonites, Lutherans, Church of Jesus Christ of Latter-day Saints (Mormons), Baptists, Presbyterians, and many independent evangelical congregations.

The Dutch Reformed Church, the largest Protestant denomination, has had close links with the government since the founding of the Dutch Republic. All the country's monarchs have been members of the Reformed Church. Congregations in South Africa, Canada, and the United States trace their roots to the Dutch church.

People of other religions in the Netherlands include Greek and Russian Orthodox, Old Catholics, Jews, Buddhists, Hindus, Muslims, and Baha'i.

Pagan Ancestors

The ancestors of the Dutch were pagans whose spirituality was based on nature and many unseen gods and lesser spirits. They were eventually converted to Christianity by courageous missionaries whose zeal overcame physical hardships and the suspicions of the local tribal leaders. Sometimes, the preaching of brotherly love was not so subtle, however. Often, behind the prayers of monks and priests was the sword. Clan chiefs saw Christianity as a way to solidify their power. In 496, for example, King Clovis I of the Franks was converted and his subjects had to follow.

Two centuries later, the Frisians were still pagans. The words of the Bible were brought to them in A.D. 700 by Willibrord, who had come from Britain. Since his ancestors probably came from the same coastal area as the Frisians at least a century earlier, he understood their temperament and was successful in his preaching. Of course, it did not hurt that he had the support of Charles Martel, a Germanic warlord who brought the Frisians under the rule of the Franks. Emperor Charlemagne finally subdued all the pagan tribes and forced Christianity upon them. It was either that or death.

To Be a People

In those days, there was no Netherlands, no "Dutch," just the far reaches of the all-encompassing Low Countries. Everyone belonged to a tribe or clan, responsible only to the strongest warrior who could protect them. However, the missionaries were the first to refer to these various tribes as a single group, lumping them all under the Latin word *gentes*, or non-Romans. Latin, the common language of the old Roman Empire, was used as much as English is today in many parts of the world. As these tribes became Christian, the idea that they could be a "people" was the start of a long evolution that eventually led to the creation of today's Netherlands.

As protection against attacks by Vikings and other enemies, the local chiefs built forts. Towns grew up

A modern Dutch Christian church

The adorned nave of Delft's Nieuwe Kerk

around the forts and monasteries and churches were constructed nearby. A wealthy merchant class developed, surrounded by all the trappings of a good lifestyle with its supporting servants, butchers, bakers, and candlestick makers. What was good for the business community became good for everyone, including the Church.

The nobles supported the merchants because they needed their money. The merchants backed the nobles because they needed their protection. And both were often aided by the Church, which required both the merchants' cash and the nobles' protection. It was no wonder that *Pax Dei*—Latin words meaning "peace of God"—meant more than spiritual benefits. It meant commercial peace too.

The people of the Low Countries became deeply religious, but their faith was tempered by practical worldly wisdom. By the Middle Ages, most people in the Low Countries were living in towns and this gave them a different outlook on life than peasants in other parts of Europe. They were independent thinkers, living under different rules. As travelers, they were able to see much more of the world than their neighbors. They were exposed to new ideas and philosophies. In the late 1300s, Geert Groote of Deventer was a saintly mystic whose principles of toleration greatly influenced attitudes of openness among those who took the time to listen.

Over the centuries, however, problems developed in the Church in Europe. Many church leaders took advantage of their high positions to amass great personal fortunes. Nobles

Huguenots in the Netherlands

John Calvin, a French theologian, was the main Protestant reformer after Martin Luther, a rebellious German monk, and Swiss churchman Huldreich Zwingli. In 1534, Calvin settled in Geneva, Switzerland. In France, his followers were called Huguenots. Most were upper-class intellectuals and middle-class merchants. In the late 1500s and early 1600s, civil wars raged between Roman Catholics and Protestants in France. Many Huguenots fled to the Netherlands, where they earned positions of authority. Their influence in politics helped lead to the overthrow of Spanish rule in the Netherlands.

allied themselves with the cardinals and bishops. They helped one another gain political and economic favors.

Their activities did not sit well with the ordinary people of the towns or with the lower ranks of clergy. They saw the cardinals and bishops becoming rich, acquiring huge estates, and even raising armies to protect their own interests.

Much to Criticize in Established Church

There was much to criticize. Johannes Brughman was a monk who did not like what he saw going on around him. He was one of many wandering preachers who encouraged the people to reject the immorality of the established Church. In the mid-1550s, he preached throughout the northern Low Countries. He was such an eloquent speaker that, even today, to say someone can "talk like Brughman" is high praise among the Dutch. Brughman was only one of many reformers who wished to see changes in the Church. But the established order considered the reformers to be heretics, or people who oppose official church doctrine, and called their preachings "heresy." Yet the reformers kept pushing their ideals. Their movement became known as the Protestant Reformation.

Persecutions Begin

During the reign of Charles V, the Low Countries remained fairly removed from the Reformation. But when followers of Martin Luther tried to influence people in the provinces, Charles began persecuting them. His son, Philip II of Spain, continued the repression. During this period, the philosophies of reformer John Calvin took hold in the northern provinces. Among other beliefs, Calvin said that people are saved only by the grace of God.

Image of John Calvin from an engraving

Many of the great nobles and the poor lower nobility used the Reformation to stir up the freedom-loving people against the king's administration and the presence of the Spanish, who happened to be Catholic. Rebellion continued, with the northern provinces asserting their independence. Calvinism then gained the ascendancy. In 1581, practice of the Catholic faith was forbidden in the Netherlands. The Catholics of the country, who made up about 40 percent of the population, were ruthlessly suppressed.

Generations passed before Catholics and Protestants could truly live together peacefully again. At the beginning of the twentieth century, Catholics went to Catholic schools and Protestants to Protestant schools. Votes went to Catholic or Protestant political parties. By the early 1950s, this self-enforced segregation was waning, and today religion is no longer an issue.

Brave Priest Dies for His Beliefs

Titus Brandsma (1881–1942) was a Carmelite priest and journalist known for his studies of mysticism and religious culture in the Low Countries. After the invasion of the Netherlands by the Germans on May 10, 1940, the Dutch hierarchy under Archbishop John de Jong soon opposed the Nazis. Catholics were forbidden to participate in Nazi Party activities that violated Catholic principles.

When the Catholic press was ordered to publish Nazi news releases and advertisements, De Jong asked Brandsma to visit newspaper editors with instructions to resist Nazi propaganda. For this, the priest was arrested. Questioned by the Nazis, Brandsma objected to Nazi policies. He strongly supported the free exercise of religion and the rights of his persecuted Jewish friends. He was accused of being a danger to the state and sent to the concentration camp at Dachau, Germany. There, Brandsma was beaten repeatedly and given an injection of a deadly drug in a so-called "medical" experiment. He died soon afterward.

On November 3, 1985, in the Basilica of St. Peter in Rome, the Catholic Church honored Titus Brandsma with the titles of Blessed and Martyr.

Religious Holidays

Saint Nicholas Day and Christmas fall on the same day every year. Dates vary from year to year for the rest.

Good Friday	March–April
Easter Sunday	March–April
Easter Monday	March–April
Ascension Day	May–June
Whitsuntide	May–June
Saint Nicholas Day	December 6
Christmas	December 25 and 26

A mosque in a new housing development in Amsterdam

Dutch Jews

Jews have a long and distinguished history in the Netherlands. Jewish traders and merchants lived in the Low Countries for centuries. An influx of Portuguese Jews fleeing persecution in the 1500s brought creative thinking, culture, and refinement to the area. Philosopher Baruch Spinoza (1632–1677) was a descendant of these immigrants. Spinoza saw mankind as part of

the order of nature, not as something special exempt from universal laws. He contributed to the development of the modern science of psychology and greatly influenced other thinkers from scientist Albert Einstein to poets like William Wordsworth.

Today, there are about 30,000 Jews in the Netherlands, mostly living in or near Amsterdam, which has a Jewish museum and two Jewish schools. One school is for six- to twelve-year-olds and the other is for twelve- to eighteen-year-olds. Most Jewish youngsters attend public schools, however. The many Jewish youth groups include Ijar, Kadima, Bne Akiva, and Habonim, and there is even a club for Hebrew speakers called Tsabar.

The story of the Dutch Jews is a special chapter in that religion's history. There is a Center for Research on Dutch Jewry at the Hebrew University of Jerusalem. Started in 1968 by Dutch Jews living in Israel, the center works with students learning more about their heritage.

Yet despite their influence on Dutch society, an estimated 100,000 Dutch Jews were hauled off to concentration camps

Jewish Safe House

The Portuguese-Jewish Synagogue in The Hague was built in 1724 by refugees fleeing religious persecution in Portugal. The Great Baliff of The Hague and other city officials were on hand when the building was dedicated. The structure is small but important in the history of the Jewish people. Its location in one of the city's most distinguished neighborhoods shows that freedom of religion has been practiced in the Netherlands over the centuries.

The city's Jewish community worshiped at the synagogue until the Netherlands was overrun by the Nazis in 1940. Most of its congregation was deported and put to death. The building was not destroyed, however, and is now considered a national landmark. The synagogue was renovated and reopened for use by the city's remaining Jews in 1976, after a ceremony attended by Queen Juliana.

and killed during World War II. That was about 95 percent of the Jewish population in the country, the highest proportion of deaths in any occupied nation during the war. Many Jews were protected and hidden by their brave non-Jewish friends. The experiences of Corrie Ten Boom, her sister Betsie, and their father, a watchmaker, are retold in Ten Boom's book *The Hiding Place*. Many of these Dutch "Righteous Persons" were jailed or killed for helping Jews.

A Dutch house converted to a mosque in Rotterdam

The number of Jewish deaths is still shocking to the Dutch, who always believed in their tradition of tolerance. In 1995, the Dutch bishops released a statement saying that the Church shared responsibility for Jewish deaths in World War II. The bishops said that because the Jews had been blamed for the death of Christ, they were often rejected as a people. This attitude may have contributed to anti-Semitism, or hostility toward Jews, during the war. The bishops' efforts at reconciliation have helped heal those wounds.

Tiny Village Lives as Memorial

The miniature village of Madurodam near The Hague opened in 1952, with re-creations of many famous buildings throughout the Netherlands. Madurodam is a memorial to the son of a Brazilian Jewish family who had served in the Dutch Army and was killed in Dachau. Proceeds go to charities that help young people.

Into the Future

Even today, new philosophies such as the Martinist Order are tested in the Netherlands. The Martinist Order, introduced in 1968, believes in an ideal society ruled by God. Its leaders are called divine commissioners. The movement started in France in the 1770s.

CHAPTER

NINE

From Painters to Punks

THE DUTCH HAVE A LONG HISTORY OF ART APPRECIATION. They love music, dance, painting, drama, and film. And nothing takes a back seat to their enjoyment of the outdoors, with its opportunities for hiking, biking, sailing, and other sports.

Vibrancy, emotion, detail, tension, color, and depth are only a few of the adjectives that describe Dutch art. While the Netherlands is tiny in size, its impact on the world's art scene has been enormous. Some of history's greatest painters were of Dutch heritage. Artist Hieronymus Bosch in *The Garden of Earthly Delights* set the tone for Dutch creativity as early as 1500 and

Opposite: **Groningen Museum**

The seventeenth century Het Loo Palace was donated in 1971 for use as a museum.

The Night Watch by
Rembrandt Van Rijn

many others followed. Probably the most famous is Rembrandt Harmenszoon van Rijn, noted for his genius in portraying people and his skill in depicting light and shadow. The son of a wealthy miller, Rembrandt was born in 1606 in Leiden. At age 18, he studied in Amsterdam and learned his craft under the direction of popular painters of that era.

Rembrandt Lives

Amsterdam looks much as it did during Rembrandt's time. Many buildings in the old city have ties to the famous artist and the people he knew. Rembrandt lived at 4–6 Jodenbreestraat, now a museum, and died at 184 Rozngracht. His first wife, Saskia van Vylenburgh, is buried in the Oude Kerk. A house at 140–142 Singel, recently restored, was the home of Frans Banningh Cocq—one of the main subjects of *The Night Watch.*

Paintings on Display

One of Rembrandt's best-known paintings is *The Night Watch,* which shows a group of soldiers. The canvas can be viewed at the Rijksmuseum in Amsterdam, along with twenty of his other works. The museum also has paintings by several of Rembrandt's students, including Govaert Flinck and Ferdinand Bol. Although he was highly respected during his life, Rembrandt never made much money. He died in poverty in 1669. Today, his works are priceless.

Jan Steen (1626–1679) used his keen sense of humor and clever eye to depict the lives of ordinary people. Steen's paintings show barking dogs, playing children, tavern scenes, and jumbled households. His works bring the seventeenth century to life. Steen's portrait of baker Arent Oostwaard and his wife is one of his most famous. His works hang in Leiden's Museum Bredius and Gallery Prins Willem V in The Hague.

Vincent van Gogh became famous only after his death. Born in 1853, Van Gogh died in 1890. But in that brief span, he painted and painted and painted, using swift, heavy strokes with a brush or pallet knife. He sold only one painting during his lifetime, but today his works are worth millions of dollars.

Johannes Vermeer (1632–1675) and Piet Mondrian (1872–1944) can also be counted among the Netherlands' most creative artists. Another painter was Anton Pieck (1920–1940), noted for his book illustrations. His brilliant imagination is showcased in fairy-tale sketches and paintings.

The journal *De Stijl* is an art publication that influenced several generations of Dutch painters, architects, and other creative types. The publication was founded by noted

Self-Portrait by Vincent van Gogh

Today's artists gather at Arti et Amicitae, a private club with a waiting list of five years.

architect J. J. P. Oud. A famous literary magazine, *Forum*, was avidly read by the Dutch creative community in the years between World Wars I and II.

Impressive Dutch Writers

Early Dutch authors are best known for their romantic novels. Elizabeth Bekker-Wolff (1738–1804) and Agatha Deken (1741–1804) wrote their popular *History of Miss Sara Burgerhart* in 1788. It tells the emotional story of a young woman forced to run away from a nasty aunt. But all was not sweetness and light. Eduard Douwes Dekker (1820–1887) wrote the hard-hitting *Max Havelaar* in 1860, telling of heavy-handed Dutch colonial rule in the East Indies.

After World War II, a trio of Dutch writers set the international publishing world buzzing. Willem Hermans, Harry Mulich, and Gerard Reve burst on the scene in the late 1940s. Their grim stories about modern Holland were unsettling, touching on how people distanced themselves from one another in a new world. Other writers, like Marga Minco, dealt with subjects that were equally disturbing. Minco's *The Bitter Herb*, written in 1957, told of the wartime persecution of Dutch Jews. She went on to write lighter fare, including numerous children's stories. *Turkish Delight*, a book written by best-selling author Jan Wolkers, was made into a movie in 1973.

Famous Dutch poets include Rhijnivis Feith (1753–1824), Willem Bilderdijk (1756–1831), Anthoni Staring (1767–1840), Dirk Coster (1887–1956), and Hendrik Marsman (1899–1940). Their writings ranged from the sentimental to the patriotic.

Dutch films are highly regarded by movie fans. Two have won Oscars for best foreign language film. *Antonia's Line*, by director Marleen Gorris, captured the award in 1995, with Mike van Diem's *Character* (right) winning in 1998.

One of the more famous Dutch playwrights was Herman Heijermans (1864–1924). A fervent socialist, he was committed to correcting injustice wherever he saw it. His plays about the hard lives of coal miners and sailors copied the speech patterns of his subjects and were easily understood by his audiences.

Concertgebouw Orchestra in Amsterdam

Love of Music

The Dutch love all kinds of music, from the smooth sounds of the Concertgebouw Orchestra to a contemporary band called Flairck, with its trendy mix of Dutch folk music and jazz. Jan Sweelinck, an Amsterdam organist, wrote hundreds of scores in the seventeenth century and his works are still being played. Hendrik Andriessen and Henriette Bosmans are among the country's leading composers today. The Netherlands has fourteen large orchestras and dozens of choirs.

People dancing to the rock group Replay during the Queen's Day festival

Think Tank Technology

In 1997, the Science and Technology Centre NewMetropolis opened in Amsterdam. The museum is packed with exhibits on energy, communication, and human relationships.

Far from the classical vein, Dutch rock bands have set a wild new pace for the fast-moving entertainment scene. It is difficult to adequately describe all the styles, but just ask any of the younger generation. Critics go wacky trying to talk about Clinch, finally settling on "grungerockpunkpop-bluescore." Altar and Eternal Solstice are two popular death metal bands who pack concert halls across Europe. GirlWonder is renowned as alternative guitarpop, with the all-women De Wow! presenting another powerful mix. Grain bills itself as a lo-fi powerpop band. Turn to the music magazines that cover the front of the newsstands and learn about Anouk, the Cheese Heads, Facing Down, Disco Fever, Freaked Cheese, and Fuzz for Brains.

Entertainment Options

The Dutch have even more entertainment possibilities to keep them busy. More than a dozen stage troupes bring classical and modern dance and drama to Dutch theatergoers. The National Ballet Company is world famous for its colorful, graceful productions. On rainy days, the Dutch can visit one of their 18 national museums or one of the 400 regional halls that showcase everything from art to natural history. The Ministry of Cultural Affairs, Recreation, and Social Welfare helps with important grants to fund films, dance, and drama.

Sports Lovers

The Dutch are active people who love sports and competition. The Netherlands Sports Museum in Lelystad, Flevoland, showcases the country's sports history. Although baseball and basketball are played in the Netherlands and have their own sports associations, football—called soccer—remains the number-one sport. The pro soccer club Ajax is always tops in international play.

The Netherlands' dream team, nicknamed "The Oranjes," qualified for the 1998 World Cup. The soccer championship, held every four years, is the world's most-watched sporting event. The 1998 games were hosted by France. Resplendent in their orange shirts and socks and white shorts, the Dutch players fought hard through their initial matches, defeating opponent after opponent, including the tough Argentines. Unfortunately, in the semifinals, they lost 4–2 to the Brazilians. The loss was heartbreaking to the Dutch because

Jari Litmanan of Ajax takes on the Udinese defense during the UEFA Cup

the two teams had battled to a 1–1 tie after 120 minutes of play at the Stadium Velodrome in Marseille. The team returned home saddened, but still heroes to their Dutch fans.

In 1974 and 1978, the Netherlands reached the World Cup final rounds. But they lost both times, making them the only team in the tournament's history to play in two finals without winning either. Dennis Bergkamp, Johan Cruff, Johan Neeskens, and Johnny Rep were among the Netherlands' greatest players in that era.

Ice Skating

Even as the winter wind blows across the icebound playing fields, the Dutch still look forward to outdoor fun. When the temperature dips below freezing, it's time to head for the canals—and ice skating. The Dutch have long been fascinated by this wintry sport, which started in the Middle Ages. Since roads were often blocked by snow, the peasants in those long-ago days found it easier to skate across the open ice. The first skates were made of cow ribs. Next came a wooden block that was eventually formed into a curved wooden skate with a steel blade. From these primitive devices came the comfortable skates we use today.

Ice-skating is a favorite pastime and sport among the Dutch.

The nobility used to sponsor ice racing on canals near their manor houses. Today, the Elevens Town Race, called the *Elfstedentocht*, is one of Europe's most famous sporting events. Weather permitting, it is held in Friesland, one of the Netherlands' northern provinces. The contestants speed through eleven towns, covering 125 miles (201 km). Due to bad weather, the grueling marathon has only been held a few times since it began in 1890, with one of the most recent years being 1997.

Along the route, vendors sell *snert*, a delicious Dutch pea soup, and hot chocolate to the spectators. The winner of the race receives a gold medal, but anyone who goes the distance is considered a real hero. It seemed like the entire nation turned out in 1986 to see Crown Prince Willem Alexander compete. He was one of 16,000 skaters that year.

Slip Sliding Away

Hans Brinker; or, the Silver Skates is a delightful children's story written by Mary Elizabeth Mapes Dodge in 1865. The story is about a Dutch brother and sister, Hans and Gretel, who wanted to win a set of silver skates in a race. The tale, which describes Dutch society of the time, relates how Gretel eventually wins the prize. It also relates how Hans works to get a famous doctor to help their father, who suffered brain damage in a fall. Dodge was born in New York City in 1831 and died in 1905.

Speedskater Gianni Romme set a world record during the 10,000-meter race in the 1998 Winter Olympics.

True to their heritage, the Dutch swept men's speed skating in the 1998 Winter Olympics in Nagano, Japan. In addition to winning the gold medal in the 10,000-meter race, the Netherlands finished with nine of the fifteen medals awarded in the men's division and two gold medals in women's speed skating. Gold medalist Gianni Romme led the Dutch rush, finishing the 10,000-meter in 13 minutes, 15.33 seconds—lopping 15.22 seconds off the world record set in the 1994 Olympics.

A Land Made for Cycling

The Dutch landscape is perfect for bicycling—great scenery along an almost-flat terrain. As a result, almost everyone in the country has at least two types of bike. One might be a lightweight racer or a rugged all-terrain bike for long-distance travel. The second bike probably has a basket on the front or back and is used for shopping at the grocery store or other short trips. Every year, more than a million bikes are sold in the Netherlands and, at present, there are an estimated 16 million bikes in the nation. Not bad for a country of 15 million people!

The Dutch ride bicycles for both recreation and transportation.

All the Big Wheels

The Dutch bike boom began in 1866 when Baron Otto Groenix van Zoelen imported some French bicycles. Soon everyone wanted to ride, but at first cycling was mostly a sport for the wealthy. However, for those who couldn't afford to buy their own "velocipede," H. H. Timmer started the first rent-a-bike business in 1869 in Amsterdam. He then organized a learn-to-ride school using French bikes. Timmer eventually linked up with Henricus Burgers, a Deventer blacksmith who was the first to make Dutch cycles. Burgers is known as the "Father of the Bike Business" in the Netherlands.

In 1871, the first Dutch biking club was organized. Others soon followed. One eventually evolved into the National Automobile Club of the Netherlands. By 1896, almost every Dutch citizen was cycling. The army even had a machine-gun-mounted bicycle battalion.

In the summer, an Eleven City Bike Tour attracts more than 15,000 participants. The course, which is similar to that of the skating competition, covers 143 miles (230 km). Cyclists come from around the world to pedal.

Bike paths are found all over the country.

Easy-to-Find Trails

Bike paths take riders to every corner of the country and it's easy to find the trails. Look for round blue signs with a white bicycle in the center. Mushroom-shaped signs tell the quickest route from one point to the next. There are even benches along the paths for tired cyclists needing a breather. The Dutch have even mingled art with cycling. You can hop on a free bike at the entrance to the De Hoge Veluwe National Park and pedal to the Kroller Muller Museum in the heart of the park. The bikeways meander past huge outdoor sculptures by Auguste Rodin and Henry Moore. At

Windsurfing on the Egmond ann Zee

the museum building, cyclists can park their bikes and go inside to look at the fabulous paintings by Pablo Picasso, Vincent van Gogh, Odilon Redon, Georges Seurat, and other famous artists.

On Land, Sea, and in the Air

The Dutch also host two of Europe's most grueling marathons. An annual Rotterdam race each April and a November run in Amsterdam draw thousands of competitors.

On the solo side, wind surfers challenge the frosty North Sea almost all year round. Wearing wetsuits, they brave the wind and waves on their narrow boards. Horseback riding, hiking, hang-gliding, parachuting, sports car racing . . . you name the sport, and the Dutch are eager fans.

CHAPTER TEN

Let's Go Dutch

Pieter and Marie Gooyer have their backpacks loaded and they're ready to roll. Their family is gearing up for a weekend biking expedition to the West Frisian Islands, one of their favorite places for a holiday. The Gooyers live in Groningen, in the far north of the Netherlands. Home is about a two-hour

Opposite: **Children play near their home along a canal in Delft.**

The city of Groningen during a national celebration

Heartrending Memorial

Rotterdam's *Monument for the Destroyed City* shows a screaming man with his hands upraised. The statue by Ossip Zadkine graphically shows the terror of a 1940 bombing raid that destroyed most of the city at the outbreak of World War II. The statue is directly behind the Maritime Museum.

drive north of Amsterdam where Grandpa and Grandma Gooyer live. The Gooyers like living in Groningen because it is within easy biking distance of some of the Netherlands' most pristine coastline and densest forests. They have often pedaled around Shiermonnikoog, another island in the North Sea criss-crossed by bike paths and hiking trails.

The previous year, the family visited Texel, the southern-most island in the chain off the Dutch coast. With their bikes carefully stowed aboard, they sailed from Rotterdam on Grandpa Gooyer's boat, *The Wooden Mermaid*. On their way out of the harbor, their little vessel was dwarfed by freighters flying flags from Liberia, Japan, and Senegal. Pieter waved to the ships' crew, who usually waved back unless they were too busy getting ready to berth at the Rotterdam docks.

Up the Western Coast

The sailboat turned at the Hoek van Holland marker and meandered up the western coast of the Netherlands. It was a leisurely, safe cruise under Grandpa Gooyer's watchful eye. Before he retired, Grandpa Gooyer had captained an oil tanker and knew all there was to know about the sea. The kids picnicked on board, their faces tingling from the salt breeze. They landed near the ferry stop at Horntje, unloaded their bikes, and set off. It was a grand week spent pedaling from village to village. Den Burg, De Koog, and De Cocksdorp are picturesque fishing ports on Texel, catering to the visitors who love the fresh winds and morning mists of the North Sea.

Texel is a great island to visit and ride bikes.

This summer's vacation promises to be just as much fun. The Gooyers waited for their annual big biking trip until after the World Cup soccer championships in June and July. Although the country lost to Brazil in the semifinal rounds the Dutch team did well in the games, which were held in France. Pieter was disappointed that his team did not make it all the way, but he went on to cheer for the French, who eventually captured the title. Some of his friends had gone to Marseilles with their parents and watched the Netherlands play Brazil. They had loads of stories to tell when they returned. But Pieter's mom and dad were saving their money for vacation so their family watched the Cup matches on television.

Pieter's room is papered with posters of the Dutch national players. He also has a ball autographed by goalie Edwin van de Sar. Van der Sar stands six feet, six inches tall (198 cm). Pieter, who is eleven years old, has a long way to grow before stretching out that far. He's a midfielder on his school team and just needs to be really fast.

Islands Are Prime Vacationland

Plenty of summertime remains to enjoy the remoteness of the Frisian islands. If this were August, however, hordes of tourists from Germany and Britain would invade the seaside. It is too crowded then for the Gooyers' liking.

The children's father, Claus, is a physics professor at the local university and their mother, Anna, is a city planner who works on projects around the world. She helped develop a management plan for Tilburg, a Dutch city near the Belgian border.

Anna was proud to learn in 1998 that a major American magazine called the town one of the world's "cities that work."

When she learned about the award, their dad took the family to celebrate at the Ugly Duck restaurant on Groningen's tree-shaded Swanstrasse. They had a great time. Pieter had a huge platter of curly kale and sausages, followed by pancakes lathered with hot butter and dappled with sugar. His mom laughed and said that if he kept eating like that he would be taller than goalie Van der Sar.

Anna Gooyer was born in Suriname, a former Dutch colony on the north coast of South America. She met Carl Gooyer while they were university students in Amsterdam. Her family, the Chamanlals, originally came to Suriname from India in 1904 and started a chain of grocery stores. Her father eventually opened an import-export business that now does business in the South American countries of Brazil, Venezuela, and Paraguay.

Public Holidays

Dates of some religious holidays vary.

New Year's Day	January 1
Good Friday	March–April
Easter Sunday	March–April
Easter Monday	March–April
Queen's Birthday	April 30
National Liberation Day	May 5
Ascension Day	May–June
Whitsuntide	May–June
Saint Nicholas Day	December 6
Christmas	December 25 and 26

A Surinamese father and a Dutch mother head this interracial family.

Return to Suriname

Every couple of years, the Gooyers return to Suriname to visit Grandpa and Grandma Chamanlal. After all the usual hugs and catch-up conversation, everyone goes exploring in the nearby rain forests. They love looking for exotic birds and animals. Anna is proud of her homeland because her relatives were active in the Suriname independence movement of the 1970s. Grandma Chamanlal also has some American Indian relatives in her background.

Pieter is small and dark like his mother, while Marie is blonde and blue-eyed like her dad. The kids think that's really neat. They feel lucky to be so "international."

Like all their friends, Pieter and Marie use their bicycles every day. It is easy to get around Groningen, a bicycle-friendly community often called "a university with a city built around it." Groningen is a culturally rich place with loads of book-stores and cafés catering to students who come from around the world. The kids love going with their parents to art shows, concerts, and plays. Besides teaching physics at the university, Carl Gooyer often lectures at schools in other parts of Europe.

Students from all over the world enjoy visiting the Netherlands.

Here Comes Saint Nicholas

December 6 is a favorite day for Dutch children. This is Saint Nicholas Day. The preceding evening, presents are placed in the children's shoes and tucked under their beds. But long before the actual holiday, preparations are being made. In late November, a ship carrying Saint Nicholas and his helper—called Black Peter—sails into the Rotterdam harbor. From there, Saint Nicholas parades through the city. Television covers his arrival with special programs. By then, all the shop windows and streets are colorfully decorated.

The real Nicholas is thought to have been from the Middle East. Perhaps he was the Bishop of Myra in Turkey in the fourth century, a man known for his charity and love of children. Today, the mythological, saintly Nicholas is kept busy as the patron of children, cities, students, and even countries. Black Peter, his servant, is thought to have been a Moor from Spain.

On this holiday, Dutch families usually have a big meal and eat loads of sweets. Special gingerbread men and spiced biscuits are favorites.

Groningen Rebuilt

Because Groningen was heavily damaged in World War II, many of its new buildings have a futuristic look. For instance, the Groningen Museum, built in 1994, is a visually delightful mix of cubes, cylinders, and squares done in pastel colors. Marie, who is twelve, likes to visit there to see all the artwork, a collection that ranges from Chinese to contemporary. She wants to become an artist because she thinks the Netherlands needs more women painters.

The shapes and colors of the
Groningen Museum impart
a very modern look.

"There's plenty of old guys in the museums," she sniffs, after touring Rembrandt's home, *Rembrandthuis*, in Amsterdam. The house holds 250 of his etchings, as well as clothing, art supplies, and other artifacts from his life. Marie works hard in her art classes because her school is having an exhibit at the town hall this coming autumn.

Ready for a Trip

"I'll have a museum of my own some day," Marie predicts. She always takes drawing materials when she goes on a biking vacation. Her colored pencils, watercolors, and paper are already packed for this summer's trip to the islands that run along the west rim of the Waddenzee.

Wadden means "mudflat" in Dutch. Actually, there is more sand here than mud in the summer. Bikers and hikers love using the tulip-lined trails that meander through the nature preserves on the islands. Hundreds of bird species live here, turning both sets of islands into a bird-watcher's paradise. Marie likes to sketch them while her dad takes photos. Pieter and his mom usually pedal on ahead, eager to see new sights.

When the traveling packs are finally loaded in the family van and the bikes fastened into their racks, the family is ready to drive to Harlingen to board the ferry. The boat will take them to the islands across the wide waters of the Waddenzee. Pieter thinks that maybe he'll be a ferry captain someday. Or maybe a tanker captain, like his grandpa. Or maybe an importer like his other grandfather. Or maybe a soccer player.

Or . . . well, he has lots of options to consider. Right now, all he has to worry about is watching the passing countryside on the way to the sea.

The scenic countryside of Texel

Timeline

Dutch History		World History	
		2500 B.C.	Egyptians build the Pyramids and Sphinx in Giza.
		563 B.C.	Buddha is born in India.
The Romans invade the Low Countries.	57 B.C.	A.D. 313	The Roman emperor Constantine recognizes Christianity.
Germanic tribes overthrow Roman regime.	A.D. 406	610	The prophet Muhammad begins preaching a new religion called Islam.
Beginning of the reign of Charlemagne, founder of the Holy Roman Empire.	768		
Viking raids.	834–1007		
Low Countries become part of the Holy Roman Empire.	925	1054	The Eastern (Orthodox) and Western (Roman) Churches break apart.
		1066	William the Conqueror defeats the English in the Battle of Hastings.
		1095	Pope Urban II proclaims the First Crusade.
Land reclamation begins.	1200s	1215	King John seals the Magna Carta.
		1300s	The Renaissance begins in Italy.
		1347	The Black Death sweeps through Europe.
Unification of the Low Countries.	1400–1558	1453	Ottoman Turks capture Constantinople, conquering the Byzantine Empire.
		1492	Columbus arrives in North America.
		1500s	The Reformation leads to the birth of Protestantism.
Beginning of the Eighty Years' War against Spain.	1568		
Pacification of Ghent is signed, establishing religious tolerance.	1576		
Union of Arras.	1579		
Union of Utrecht.	1581		
Twelve Years' Truce between the Dutch Republic and Spain.	1609–1621		
Dutch colonial expansion.	From 1620s		
William III and Mary Stuart become joint rulers of the Netherlands and England.	1689		
		1776	The Declaration of Independence is signed.

Dutch History

France declares war on Britain and the Dutch Republic.	1793
France occupies the Dutch Republic.	1795
Louis Napoleon, brother of Napoleon Bonaparte, becomes king of Holland.	1806
The Kingdom of Holland is annexed to France.	1810
Independence restored by Congress of Vienna; Belgium and Luxembourg added to Dutch territory.	1815
Belgium gains independence from the Netherlands.	1830
New Constitution brings greater religious freedom.	1848
Barrier Dam completed; land reclamation considerably enlarges the surface area of the Netherlands.	1932
Occupation by German forces.	1940–45
The Netherlands liberated by Canadian and Polish troops. The Netherlands becomes a member of the United Nations.	1945
Transfer of sovereignty to Indonesia. The Netherlands becomes a member of NATO.	1949
Disastrous floods in the southern coastal region kill nearly 2,000 people.	1953
Charter of the Kingdom of the Netherlands establishes the present-day composition of the nation.	1954
The Netherlands is a founding member of the European Economic Community.	1956
Delta Project initiated. First dams and moveable storm-surge barriers constructed.	1958
Netherlands grants independence to Suriname.	1975
The States-General of the Netherlands ratifies the Maastricht Treaty.	1992
Severe flooding causes evacuation of 250,000 people and $1 billion in damage.	1995
Completion of the Delta Project.	1997

World History

1789	The French Revolution begins.
1865	The American Civil War ends.
1914	World War I breaks out.
1917	The Bolshevik Revolution brings Communism to Russia.
1929	Worldwide economic depression begins.
1939	World War II begins, following the German invasion of Poland.
1957	The Vietnam War starts.
1989	The Berlin Wall is torn down as Communism crumbles in Eastern Europe.
1996	Bill Clinton re-elected U.S. president.

Fast Facts

Official name: *Koninkrijk der Nederlanden*
(Kingdom of the Netherlands)

Capital: Amsterdam

Oude Harbor

NETHERLANDS
- Cities of over 100,000 people
- Smaller cities and towns
- Divisional capitals
- Canals

0   40 miles
0   60 kilometers

NORTH SEA

West Frisian Islands

Waddenzee

Groningen
GRONINGEN
Leeuwarden
FRIESLAND
Assen
DRENTHE

NOORD-HOLLAND
IJsselmeer (Zuider Zee)
FLEVOLAND
Alkmaar
Lelystad
Zwolle
OVERIJSSEL
Deventer
Enschede

Haarlem
Amsterdam
Apeldoorn

ZUID-HOLLAND
Leiden
Old Rhine
Utrecht
GELDERLAND
Arnhem
UTRECHT
Lower Rhine
The Hague
Delft
Lek
Nijmegen
Rotterdam
Maas
ZEELAND
Dordrecht

Middelburg
NOORD-BRABANT
Breda
's Hertogenbosch
Tilburg
Eindhoven
Terneuzen
LIMBURG
Rhine

Lys
Brussels
Maastricht
BELGIUM
Meuse
GERMANY

NETHERLANDS

LUXEMBOURG

Hortus Botanicus

Flag of the Netherlands

Skates

Official language:	Dutch
Official religion:	None, but the Dutch State has long had a close association with the Reformed Church.
Year of founding:	1579
Founder:	William of Orange
National anthem:	*Wilhelmus van Nassouwe* ("William of Nassau")
Government:	Constitutional monarchy
Chief of state:	King or queen
Head of government:	Prime minister
Area:	16,033 square miles (41,522 square kilometers) total; land surface: 13,104 square miles (33,939 sq km)
Latitude and longitude of geographic center:	52° 30' North, 5° 45' East
Land and water borders:	The North Sea on the west and north, Germany on the east, and Belgium on the south
Highest elevation:	Vaalser Berg, 1,053 ft (321 m) above sea level
Lowest elevation:	Prins Alexander Polder, 22 feet (6.7 m) below sea level
Average temperature extremes:	37°F (3°C) in January; 62°F (17°C) in July
Average precipitation:	29 inches (74 cm)

A cheese market

Amsterdam

National population (1997 est.):	15,653,091

Population of largest cities:

Amsterdam (1998 est.)	718,175
Rotterdam (1997 est.)	598,521

Famous landmarks:

- ▶ *Anne Frank House* (Amsterdam)
- ▶ *Palace Het Loo* (Apeldoorn)
- ▶ *The Ridderzaal* (The Hague)
- ▶ *The Peace Palace*, home of the International Court of Justice (The Hague)

Industry: Metals, machinery, chemicals, oil refinery, diamond cutting, electronics, tourism

Currency: The guilder (in 1999, U.S.$1 = 2.07 guilders). Conversion to Euro, a common currency for all members of the European Union, begins in 1999.

Systems of weights and measures: Metric system

Literacy: 99 percent (1993 estimate)

Common Dutch words and phrases:

Dag!	Good day! (used both in greeting and to say good-bye)
als't u blieft	if you please (used as both "please" and "you're welcome")
dank u wel	thank you
lekker	delicious; wonderful
tot ziens!	See you later!

Queen Beatrix

Famous people:

Tobias M. C. Asser *Law professor*	(1838–1913)
Queen Beatrix *Queen of the Netherlands*	(1938–)
Erasmus Desiderius *Priest and philosopher*	(1466–1536)
Vincent van Gogh *Painter*	(1853–1890)
Herman Heijermans *Playwright*	(1864–1924)
Anton van Leeuwenhoek *Scientist*	(1632–1723)
Etta Lubina Johanna Palm *Political feminist*	(1743– ?)
Rembrandt van Rijn *Painter*	(1606–1669)
William of Orange *Founder of the Dutch Republic*	(1533–1584)

Vincent van Gogh

To Find Out More

Nonfiction

▶ Ippisch, Hanneke. *Sky: A True Story of Courage During World War II.* East Rutherford, N.J.: Troll Communications, 1998.

▶ Pescio, Claudio. *Rembrandt and Seventeenth-Century Holland: The Dutch Nation and Its Painters.* Lincolnwood, Ill.: Peter Bedrick Books, 1995.

▶ Seth, Ronald. *The Netherlands.* Broomall, Pa.: Chelsea House Publications, 1997.

▶ Seward, Pat. *Netherlands.* Tarrytown, N.Y.: Marshall Cavendish Corp., 1995.

▶ Van Fenema, Joyce. *Netherlands.* Milwaukee: Gareth Stevens, 1998.

Fiction

▶ Attema, Martha. *A Time to Choose.* Custer, Wash.: Orca Book Publications, 1995.

▶ Van Stockum, Hilda. *A Day on Skates: The Story of a Dutch Picnic.* Fort Collins, Colo.: Ignatius Press, 1995.

▶ Vos, Ida. *Hide and Seek.* Madison, Wis.: Demco Media Distribution, 1995.

▶ Vos, Ida, Terese Edelstein, and Inez Smidt. *Dancing on the Bridge of Avignon.* Westminster, Md.: Houghton Mifflin, 1995.

Websites

▶ **City of Amsterdam**
http://www.amsterdam.nl/adam_
eng.html
*In both Dutch and English, this site
on Amsterdam includes departments
for current events and news, the
city government, facts and figures,
the economy, tourism, history, and
a guided virtual tour.*

▶ **The European Union in
the United States**
http://www.eurunion.org
*The official European Union site con-
tains an EU profile and information on
resources, web sites, member states,
policies and legislation, news, publications, and offices in the U.S.*

▶ **Official Holland Site—
Netherlands Board of Tourism**
http://www.visitholland.com/
index.html
*This official site of Holland displays
beautiful graphics, as well as information about family vacations, bicycle
routes, cultural attractions, history and
the coast, tourist boards, and attractions and events for each city.*

▶ **Royal Netherlands Embassy**
http://www.netherlands-
embassy.org/index.html
*The official site of the Netherlands
embassy displays information on its
many offices, including agriculture,
economy, health, politics, and science.
Also contains links to Dutch web
sites, a search engine, and contact
information.*

Organizations and Embassies

▶ **Royal Netherlands Embassy**
4200 Linnean Ave., NW
Washington, DC 20008
(202) 244-5300

▶ **European Union**
Delegation of the European
Commission to the U.S.
2300 M Street NW
Washington, DC 20037
(202) 862-9500

Index

Page numbers in *italics* indicate illustrations

Meet the Author

ARTIN HINTZ is a member of the Society of American Travel Writers. He lives in Milwaukee, Wisconsin, but travels throughout the world researching stories for books and articles.

A former newspaper reporter and editor, Hintz has written extensively about Europe and the Americas. He has published over thirty books and has contributed to dozens of guidebooks. In addition to *The Netherlands*, he has written *The Bahamas*, *Haiti*, *Poland*, and *Israel* for the new Enchantment of the World series. Hintz is also the author of several books in the America the Beautiful series.

Hintz is publisher of *The Irish American Post*, a news journal covering Irish and Irish American culture, sports, entertainment, business, land, and politics.

In addition to speaking to Dutch business, tourism, and cultural leaders while researching this book, Hintz dug deep into library archives. There, he studied the country's history and its famous personalities. He read about the nation's major cities, checked out books on artists, and read stories dealing with the Dutch. He poured over governmental economic reports, studied documents dealing with Dutch social services, checked over tourism publications, and surfed the Internet in search of interesting facts.

He even ate various Dutch cheeses, munched herring, and nibbled pastries . . . just for taste tests, of course. However, he has yet to try on a pair of wooden shoes.

Photo Credits

Photographs ©:

AKG London: 41, 46;
AllSport USA: 112 (Chaun Botterill), 110 (Stu Forster);
AP/Wide World Photos: 47;
Archive Photos: 55 (Reuters/Boudwijn Benting), 52, 133 top (Reuters/Jasper Juinen);
Art Resource, NY: 105 top, 133 bottom (Giraudon);
Bart van Overbeeke: 88 top; Bert Otten: 117; Bridgeman Art Library International Ltd., London/New York: 35 (PFA109556 *Portrait of a West Friesian Couple with Their Two Children* by Mijnerts Herman Doncker, Phillips, The International Fine Art Auctioneers/Private Collection), 124 (NAT36106 *St. Nicholas and a black helper*, Dutch card/Private Collection);
Brown Brothers: 59 bottom;
Christian Kohler: 90, 93, 100, 114, 122;
Corbis-Bettmann: 45 (Novosti), 44 (UPI), 43, 95;
E.T. Archive: 34, 38;
Envision: 89 (Amy Reichman);
Gamma-Liaison, Inc.: 111, 131 bottom (Emile Luider/Rapho), 27 (X. Richer);
H. Armstrong Roberts, Inc.: 7 bottom, 74 (Geisser), 83 (Geopress), 62 (R. Kord), 118 (C. May), 72 (H. Armstrong Roberts), 2, 7 top, 30, 69, 79, 132 bottom (M. Thonig);
John Elk III: 50, 53, 77, 94;
National Geographic Image Collection: 80, 81, 103 (Nathan Benn), 78, 105 bottom (Farrell Grehan);
Netherlands Board of Tourism: 88 bottom (D. Bartruff), 107 bottom;
New England Stock Photo: 91, 116 (Marc A. Auth);

North Wind Picture Archives: 37, 97;
Photo Researchers: 40 (Archiv), 19 (Kees van den Berg), 9 (Tetrel/Explorer), 108 (Farrell Grehan), 33 top (Adam Jones), 13 (Robin Laurance), 68 (Sam C. Pierson), 87 (Giulio Veggi/White Star), 33 bottom (Roger Wilmshurst);
Photofest: 107 top;
Photophile: 82;
Stock Montage, Inc.: 21;
Superstock, Inc.: 104 (Rijksmuseum Vincent Van Gogh, Amsterdam, Netherlands), 96 (Palazzo Barberini, Rome Italy/E. T. Archive, London), 11, 22, 25, 26, 49, 60, 67, 85 bottom, 98, 101;
Tiofoto: 115 (Lars Dahlstrom), 23 (Hiroshi Higuchi), 17, 73 bottom, 14, 48, 58, 63, 65, 123, 130 (Nils-Johan Norenlind), 15, 16 (Jan Rietz);
Tony Stone Images: 51 (John Elk), 73 top (Johan Elzenga), cover, 6 (John Lawrence), 71 (Cathlyn Melloan), 70, 132 top (Maarten Udema);
Viesti Collection, Inc.: 28, 131 top (Stanislas Fautre/Ask Images), 59 top, 85 top, 102, 125 (The Picture Box), 119, 127 (The Picture Box/Jaap Bongers), 12 (Richard Pasley), 76 (Joe Viesti);
Visuals Unlimited: 32 (Lindholm), 31 (Joe McDonald);
Wolfgang Käehler: 8 (Provia);
Woodfin Camp & Associates: 24 (Nathan Benn), 20, 113 (Mike Yamashita).

Maps by Joe LeMonnier